# WAT
# THE

## BY LILLIAN HELLMAN

DRAMATISTS
PLAY SERVICE
INC.

*Watch on the Rhine* was produced in New York by Herman Shumlin with the following cast:

Anise ........................................ Eda Heinemann
Fanny Farrelly ................................ Lucile Watson
Joseph ....................................... Frank Wilson
David Farrelly ................................ John Lodge
Marthe de Brancovis .......................... Helen Trenholme
Teck de Brancovis ............................ George Coulouris
Sara Muller .................................. Mady Christians
Joshua Muller ................................ Peter Fernandez
Bodo Muller .................................. Eric Roberts
Babette Muller ............................... Anne Blyth
Kurt Muller .................................. Paul Lukas

The scene of the play is the living room of the Farrelly country house, about twenty miles from Washington. The time is late spring, 1940.

### ACT I
Early on a Wednesday morning.

### ACT II
About ten days later.

### ACT III
A half hour later.

# WATCH ON THE RHINE

## ACT I

SCENE: *The living-room of the Farrelly house, about twenty miles from Washington, D. C., on a warm July morning.*

*Center stage are large French doors leading to an elevated open terrace. On the terrace are chairs, tables, a large table for dining. Some of this furniture we can see: most of it is on the left side of the terrace, beyond our sight.* L. *stage is an arched entrance, leading to the oval reception hall.* R. *stage is a door leading to a library. The Farrelly house was built in the early 19th century. It has space, simplicity, style. The living-room is large. Upstage* L., *a piano, downstage* L., *a couch, downstage* R., *a couch and chairs, upstage a few smaller chairs. Four or five generations have furnished this room and they have all been people of taste. There are no styles, no periods; the room has never been refurnished. Each careless aristocrat has thrown into the room what he or she brought home when grown-up. Therefore the furniture is of many periods: the desk is English, the couch is Victorian, some of the pictures are modern, some of the ornaments French. The room has too many things in it: vases, clocks, miniatures, boxes, china animals. On the* L. *wall is a large portrait of a big kind-faced man in an evening suit of 1900. On another wall is a large, very ugly landscape. The room is crowded. But it is cool and clean and its fabrics and woods are in soft colors.*

AT RISE: ANISE, *a thin Frenchwoman of about sixty, in a dark housekeeper's dress, is standing at a table, sorting mail. She takes the mail from a small basket, holds each letter to the light, reads each postal card, then places them in piles. On the terrace,* JOSEPH, *a tall middle-aged negro butler, wheels a breakfast wagon. As he appears,*

5

FANNY FARRELLY *comes on from the hall. She is a hand-some woman of about sixty-three. She has on a fancy, good-looking dressing-gown.*
NOTE: L. *and* R. *are the audience's left and right.*

FANNY. (*Stops to watch* ANISE. *Sees* JOSEPH *moving about on terrace. Calls.*) Joseph!

JOSEPH. Yes'm.

FANNY. (*To* ANISE.) 'Morning.

ANISE. (*Continues examining mail.*) Good morning, Madame.

JOSEPH. (*Comes to terrace door.*) Yes'm?

FANNY. Everybody down?

JOSEPH. No'm. Nobody. I'll get your tea. (*Starts off* R. *on terrace. He returns to breakfast wagon on terrace.*)

FANNY. (*Calling off* R.) Mr. David isn't down yet? (*Coming into room toward* ANISE, *crosses to sofa* L.—*sits* L. *end.*) But he knows he is to meet the train.

JOSEPH. (*Comes in from terrace with cup of tea. To top of step* R. *of* FANNY.) He's got plenty of time, Miss Fanny. The train ain't in till noon.

FANNY. Breakfast is at nine o'clock in this house and will be until the day after I die. Ring the bell.

JOSEPH. (*Goes* D. L. *to* FANNY; *gives her tea.*) But it ain't nine yet, Miss Fanny. It's eight-thirty.

FANNY. Well, put the clocks up to nine and ring the bell.

JOSEPH. (*Crosses* U. C. *toward door.*) Mr. David told me not to ring it any more. He says it's got too mean a ring, that bell. It disturbs folks. (*Stops at sound of her voice and turns.*)

FANNY. That's what it was put there for. I like to disturb folks.

JOSEPH. Yes'm. (*Goes* U. S. *through terrace door and off* R.)

FANNY. You slept well, Anise. You were asleep before I could dismantle myself.

ANISE. I woke several times during the night.

FANNY. Did you? Then you were careful not to stop snoring. We must finally get around (ANISE *brings letters to* FANNY.) to re-arranging your room. (ANISE *hands her three or four letters.* FANNY *puts down tea.*) Even when you don't snore, it irritates me. (ANISE *crosses* D. L., *sits in armchair, opens and reads French newspaper.* FANNY *begins to open mail, to read it. After a moment.*) What time is it?

ANISE. It is about eight-thirty. Joseph just told you.

6

FANNY. I didn't hear him. I'm nervous. Naturally. (*Continues to read.*) My mail looks dull. (*Looking at letter in her hand. Still reading.*) Jenny always tells you a piece of gossip three times, as if it grew fresher with the telling. Did you put flowers in their rooms?

ANISE. Certainly.

FANNY. David ought to get to the station by eleven-thirty.

ANISE. (*Patiently.*) The train does not draw in until ten minutes past noon.

FANNY. But it might come in early. (*Irritably.*) It might. Don't argue with me about everything. What time is it?

ANISE. (*Looking at watch.*) It's now twenty-seven minutes before nine. It will be impossible to continue telling you the time every three minutes from now until Miss Sara arrives. I think you are having a nervous breakdown. Compose yourself.

FANNY. It's been twenty years. Any mother would be nervous. If your daughter were coming home and you hadn't seen her, and a husband, *and* grandchildren ——

ANISE. I do not say that it is wrong to be nervous. I, too, am nervous. I say only that you are.

FANNY. Very well. I heard you. I say that I am. (*She taps her fingers on the chair, goes back to reading her letter. Looks up.*) Jenny's still in California. She's lost her lavalliere again. Birdie Chase's daughter is still faire l'amouring with that actor. Tawdry, Jenny says it is. An actor. Fashions in sin change. In my day, it was Englishmen. I don't understand infidelity. (*Puts down letters beside her and picks up teacup.*) If you love a man, then why? If you don't love him, then why stay with him? (*Without turning, she points over her head to* JOSHUA FARRELLY'S *portrait over mantel. Sips tea.*) Thank God, I was in love. I thought about Joshua last night. Three grandchildren. He would have liked that. I hope I will. (*Sips tea again and puts down cup. Points to other letters.*) Anything in anybody else's mail?

ANISE. Advertisements for Mr. David, and legal things. For our Count and Countess, there is nothing but what seems an invitation to a lower-class Embassy tea, and letters asking for bills to get paid.

FANNY. That's every morning. (*Thoughtfully.*) In the six weeks the Balkan nobility have been with us, they seem to have run up a great many bills.

7

ANISE. (FANNY *picks up tea*.) Yes. I told you that. Then, there was a night-letter for Mr. David.

(*A very loud, very unpleasant bell begins to ring*.)

FANNY. (*Through the noise*.) Really? From whom?
ANISE. From her. I took it on the telephone, and ——

(*Bell drowns out her voice*.)

FANNY. Who is " her " ? (*Bell becomes very loud*.) Go tell him to stop that noise ——
ANISE. (*Crosses to terrace, calling off* R.) Joseph! Stop that bell. Miss Fanny says to stop it. (*She crosses back to chair* D. L. *and sits*.)
JOSEPH. (*Calls*.) Miss Fanny said to start it.
FANNY. (*Shouts out to him*.) I didn't tell you to hang yourself with it.
JOSEPH. (*Appears on terrace from* R.) I ain't hung. Your breakfast is ready. (*Disappears off* R.)
FANNY. (*To* ANISE.) Who is " her " ?
ANISE. That Carter woman from Lansing, Michigan.
FANNY. Oh, my. Is she back in Washington again? What did the telegram say?
ANISE. It said the long sickness of her dear Papa had terminated in full recovery.
FANNY. That's too bad.
ANISE. She was returning, and would Mr. David come for dinner a week from Thursday? " Love," it said, " to you and your charming mother." (*To* FANNY.) That's you. I think Miss Carter from Lansing, Michigan, was unwise in attending the illness of her Papa.
FANNY. I hope so. Why?
ANISE. (*Shrugs*.) There is much winking of the eyes going on between our Countess and Mr. David.
FANNY. (*Eagerly*.) I know that. Anything new happen?
ANISE. (*Too innocently*.) Happen? I don't know what you mean.
FANNY. You know damned well what I mean.
ANISE. That? Oh, no, I don't think that.
JOSEPH. (*Appears at terrace door*.) The sausage cakes is shrinking.
FANNY. (*Rises, shrieks, crosses* R. *taking letters*.) I want everybody down here immediately. (*To* JOSEPH.) Is the car ready? (JOSEPH *nods. To* ANISE.) Did you order a good dinner? (*At hall*

8

*door.*) David! (DAVID FARRELLY, *a pleasant-looking young man of thirty-nine, comes in from the entrance hall.*) Oh!

DAVID. (*Crossing the room. Crosses to mail table.*) Good morning, everybody.

ANISE. (*To* FANNY.) Everything is excellent. You have (JOSEPH *crosses* D. L. *to sofa, picking up teacup.*) been asking the same questions for a week. You have made the kitchen very nervous.

(FANNY *crosses behind sofa* R. *to* U. R. C.)

DAVID. (*Examining mail. To* JOSEPH.) Why did you ring that air raid alarm again?

JOSEPH. (*Crosses* U. R. C., *crossing* DAVID.) Ain't me, Mr. David. I don't like no noise. Miss Fanny told me. (*Exits through terrace door* U. R. C.)

FANNY. (*Crosses to* DAVID.) Good morning, David.

DAVID. (*Calls to* JOSEPH, *who has gone.*) Tell Fred to leave the car. I'll drive to the station. (*To* FANNY, *half amused, half annoyed. Begins to read his mail.*) Mama, I think we'll fix up the chicken house for you as a playroom. We'll hang the room with bells and you can go into your second childhood in the proper privacy. (*He kisses her cheek and turns back to his mail.*)

FANNY. I find it very interesting. You sleep soundly, you rise at your usual hour—although your sister, whom you haven't seen in years, is waiting at the station ——

DAVID. She is not waiting at the station. *The train does not come in until ten minutes past twelve.*

FANNY. (*Airily.*) It's almost that now.

ANISE. (*Turns to look at her.*) Really, Miss Fanny, contain yourself. It is twenty minutes before nine.

DAVID. And I have *not* slept soundly. And I've been up since six o'clock.

FANNY. (*Turns up and* R.) Really? The Balkans aren't down yet. Where are they?

DAVID. I don't know.

ANISE. (*Picks up bag, crosses* R.) There is nothing in your mail, Mr. David, only the usual advertisements.

DAVID. And for me, that is all that is ever likely to come—here.

ANISE. (*Stops* R. *before sofa. Haughtily, as she starts toward hall.*) I cannot, of course, speak for Miss Fanny. (*Crosses* R. *to door and stops.*) I have never opened a letter in my life.

9

DAVID. I know. You don't have to. For you, they fly open.

FANNY. (*Giggles.*) It's true. (*Two steps toward* ANISE *to back of chair* R. C.) You're a snooper, Anise. (ANISE *exits* R. FANNY *talks as* ANISE *moves out. Turns to* DAVID.) I rather admire it. It shows an interest in life. (*She looks up at* JOSHUA'S *portrait.*) You know, I've been lying awake most of the night: wondering what Papa would have thought about Sara (DAVID *looks at her.*) and —— He'd have been very pleased, wouldn't he? I always find myself wondering what Joshua would have felt ——

DAVID. Yes. But maybe it would be just as well if you didn't expect me to be wondering about it, too. (DAVID *takes letters, crosses* R., *puts them on secretary,* U. R.) I wasn't married to him, Mama. He was just my father.

FANNY. My. You got up on the wrong side of the bed. (*She moves to mail table, points to mail.*) The bills are for our noble guests. Interesting—how (*Crosses* R. *to* DAVID.) many there are every morning. How much longer are they going to be with us?

DAVID. (*Without looking at her.*) I don't know.

FANNY. It's been six weeks. Now that Sara and her family are coming, even this house might be a little crowded —— (*Starts* L. *He looks up· at her. Quickly.*) I know I invited them. I felt sorry for Marthe, (*Moves to* R. *of piano keyboard.*) and Teck rather amused me. He plays good cribbage, and he tells good jokes. But that's not enough for a lifetime guest. If you've been urging her to stay, I wish you'd stop it. (*Turns to* DAVID.) They haven't any money; all right, lend them some ——

DAVID. I have been urging them to stay?

FANNY. I'm not so old I don't recognize flirting when I see it.

DAVID. But you're old enough not to be silly.

FANNY. I'm not silly. I'm charming.

(MARTHE DE BRANCOVIS, *an attractive woman of thirty-one or two, enters from* R.)

MARTHE. Good morning, Fanny. 'Morning, David.

FANNY. (U. C. *at terrace door.*) Good morning, Marthe.

DAVID. (*Warmly.*) Good morning.

MARTHE. (*Crosses* U. R. *to* R. *of* FANNY.) Fanny, darling, couldn't you persuade yourself to let me have a tray in bed and some cotton for my ears?

DAVID. (*Steps up to doorstep.*) Certainly not. My father ate breakfast at nine, and whatever my father did ——

FANNY. (*In* U. C. *door. Carefully, to* DAVID.) There was a night-letter for you from that Carter woman in Lansing, Michigan. She is returning and you are to come to dinner next Thursday. (*As she exits on terrace.*) C-A-R-T-E-R. (*Pronounces it carefully.*) Lansing, Michigan.

DAVID. (*Laughs.*) I know how to spell Carter, but thank you. (FANNY *exits through terrace door and off* U. R. DAVID *looks up at* MARTHE.) Do you understand my mother?

MARTHE. (*Crosses* C.) Sometimes.

DAVID. Miss Carter was done for your benefit.

MARTHE. (*Smiles.*) That means she has guessed that I would be jealous. And she has guessed right.

DAVID. (*Looks at her.*) Jealous?

MARTHE. (*Gaily.*) I know I have no right to be but I am. And Fanny knows it.

DAVID. (*Carelessly.*) Don't pay any attention to Mama. (*Crosses below* MARTHE *to liquor table* U. R. C.) She has a sure instinct for women I like, and she begins to hammer away early. Marthe— (*Goes to decanter on side table.*) I'm going to have a drink. I haven't had a drink before breakfast since the day I took my bar examination. (*Pours himself a drink, gulps it down.*) What's it going to be like to stand on a station platform and see your sister after all these years—I'm afraid, I guess.

MARTHE. Why?

DAVID. I don't know. Afraid she won't like me —— (*Shrugs.*) We were very fond of each other, but it's been a long time.

MARTHE. I remember Sara. Mama brought me one day when your Father was stationed in Paris. I was about six and Sara was about fifteen and you were ——

DAVID. (*Two steps toward* L.) You were a pretty little girl.

MARTHE. Do you really remember me? You never told me before. Mama and Fanny went off to gossip, and you and Sara and Anise and I sat stiffly in the garden; and I felt much too young. And then your Mama began to yell at my Mama ——

FANNY. (*Yelling from terrace off* R.) David! Come to breakfast.

DAVID. (*As if he had not been listening.*) You know, I've never met Sara's husband. Mama did. I think the first day Sara met him, in Munich. Mama didn't like the marriage much in those days—and Sara didn't care, and Mama didn't like Sara not caring. Mama cut up about it, bad.

MARTHE. Why?

11

DAVID. Probably because they didn't let her arrange it. Why does Mama ever act badly? She doesn't remember ten minutes later.

MARTHE. Wasn't Mr. Muller poor?

DAVID. Oh, Mama wouldn't have minded that. If only they'd come home and let her fix their lives for them —— (*Smiles:*) But Sara didn't want it that way.

MARTHE. (*Crosses to mail table,* U. L. C.) You'll have a house full of refugees—us and ——

DAVID. (*Smiles.*) Are you and Teck refugees? (*More toward her.*) I'm not sure I know what you're refugees from.

MARTHE. (*Turns to* DAVID.) From Europe.

DAVID. From what Europe?

MARTHE. (*Smiles, shrugs.*) I don't know. I don't know myself, really. Just Europe. (*Steps toward* DAVID. *Quickly, comes to him.*) Sara will like you. I like you. (*Laughs.*) That doesn't make sense, does it?

(*On her speech,* TECK DE BRANCOVIS *appears in hall,* R. *He is a good-looking man of about forty-five. She stops quickly.*)

TECK. (*To* MARTHE *and* DAVID.) Good morning.

(*The bell gives an enormous ring.*)

DAVID. (*Goes to terrace.*) Good morning, Teck. For years I've been thinking they were coming for Mama with a net. I'm giving up hope. I may try catching her myself. (*Disappears, calling.*) Mama! Stop that noise. (*Exits through terrace door, goes off* R.)

(MARTHE *crosses to* R. C. *above chair.*)

TECK. I wonder if science has a name for women who enjoy noise. (*Goes to table, picks up his mail.*) Many mistaken people, Marthe, seem to have given you many charge accounts.

MARTHE. (*Crosses toward him, extends hand for mail.*) The Countess de Brancovis. That still does it. It would be nice to be able to pay bills again —— (*Crosses to front of sofa* L.)

TECK. Do not act as if I refuse to pay them, Marthe. (*Crosses to* R. *end of sofa* L.) I did not sleep well last night. I was worried. (MARTHE *sits on sofa* L.) We have eighty-seven dollars in American Express checks. (*Pleasantly, looking at her.*) That's all we have.

MARTHE. (*Shrugs, opening and reading letters.*) Maybe something will turn up. It's due.

TECK. (*Carefully.*) David? (*Then, as she turns to look at him.*) The other relatives will arrive this morning? (*Crosses* R. *to* U. C.)

MARTHE. Yes.

TECK. (U. C.—*looks out on terrace.*) I think Madame Fanny and Mr. David may grow weary of accents and charity guests. Or is the husband (*Turns to her.*) of the sister a rich one?

MARTHE. No. He's poor. He had to leave Germany in '33. (MARTHE *reads mail throughout this exchange.*)

TECK. A Jew?

MARTHE. No. I don't think so.

TECK. Why did he have to leave Germany?

MARTHE. (*Still reading.*) Oh, I don't know, Teck. He's an anti-Nazi.

TECK. A political?

MARTHE. No, I don't think so. He was an engineer. I don't know. I don't know much about him.

TECK. (*Crosses to* R. *end of sofa* L.) Did you sleep well?

MARTHE. Yes. Why not?

TECK. Money does not worry you?

MARTHE. It worries me very much. But I just lie still now and hope. I'm glad to be here. (*Shrugs.*) Maybe something good will happen. (*Looks at* TECK.) We've come to the end of a road. That's been true for a long time. Things will have to go one way or the other. Maybe they'll go well, for a change.

TECK. I have not come to the end of any road.

MARTHE. (*Looks at him, smiles.*) No? (*Rises, crosses front of* TECK *toward window* U. R. C.) I admire you.

TECK. I'm going into Washington tonight. Phili has a poker game every Wednesday evening. He has arranged for me to join it.

MARTHE. (*After a pause.*) Have you been seeing Phili?

TECK. Once or twice. Why not? Phili and I are old friends. He may prove useful. I do not want to stay in this country forever.

MARTHE. (*Crosses to* TECK.) You can't leave them alone. Your favorite dream, isn't it, Teck, that they will let you play with them again. I don't think they will and I don't think you should be seeing Phili or that you should be seen at the Embassy.

TECK. (*Smiles.*) You have political convictions now?

MARTHE. I don't know what I have. I've never liked Nazis, as you know, and you should have had enough of them. They seem to have had enough of you, God knows. It would be just as well to admit they are smarter than you are, and let them alone.

TECK. (*Looking at her carefully, after a minute.*) That is interesting.

MARTHE. What is interesting?

TECK. I think you are trying to say something to me. What is it?

MARTHE. That you ought not to be at the Embassy, and that it's insane to play cards in a game with Von Seitz with eighty-seven dollars in your pocket. I don't think he'd like your not being able to pay up. Suppose you lose?

TECK. I shall try not to lose.

MARTHE. But if you do lose and can't pay, it will be all over Washington in an hour. (*Points to terrace.*) They'll find out about it, and we'll be out of here when they do.

TECK. I think I want to be out of here. I find that I do not like the picture of you and our host.

MARTHE. (D. S. *few steps to back of chair* C. *Carefully.*) There is no picture, as you put it, to like or dislike.

TECK. Not yet? I am glad to hear that. (*Comes slowly toward her. Crosses* R. *to* L. *of* MARTHE.) Marthe, you understand that I am not really a fool? You understand that it is unwise to calculate me that way?

MARTHE. (*Slowly, as if it were an effort.*) Yes, I understand that. And I understand that I am getting tired. Just plain tired. The whole thing's too much for me. I've always meant to ask you, since you play on so many sides, why we don't come out any better. I've always wanted to ask you how it happened. (*Sharply.*) I'm tired, see? And I just want to sit down. Just to sit down in a chair and stay.

TECK. (*Carefully.*) Here?

MARTHE. I don't know. Any place ——

TECK. You have thus arranged it with David?

MARTHE. I've arranged nothing.

TECK. But you are trying, eh? I think no. I would not like that. Do not make any arrangements, Marthe, I may not allow you to carry them through. (*Smiles.*) Come to breakfast now. (*He passes her, disappears on terrace. She stands still and thoughtful. Then she, too, moves to terrace, disappears.*)

(JOSEPH *appears on terrace, carrying a tray toward the unseen breakfast table. The stage is empty. After a minute there are sounds of footsteps in the hall.* SARA MULLER *appears in the door-*

14

way, comes toward the middle of the room as if expecting to find somebody, stops, looks around, begins to smile. Behind her in the doorway are three CHILDREN; behind them, KURT MULLER. They stand waiting, watching SARA. SARA is forty-one or two, a good-looking woman, with a well-bred, serious face. She is very badly dressed. Her dress is too long, her shoes were bought a long time ago and have no relation to the dress, and the belt of her dress has become untied and is hanging down. She looks clean and dowdy. As she looks around the room, her face is gay and surprised. Smiling, without turning, absently, she motions to the children and KURT. Slowly, the children come in. BODO MULLER, a boy of nine, comes first. He is carrying coats. Behind him, carrying two cheap valises, is JOSHUA MULLER, a boy of fourteen. Behind him is BABETTE MULLER, a pretty little girl of twelve. They are dressed for a much colder climate. They come forward, look at their mother, then move to a couch. Behind them is KURT MULLER, a large, powerful, German-looking man of about forty-three. He is carrying a shabby valise and a briefcase. He stands watching SARA. JOSHUA puts down the valises, goes to his father, takes the valise from KURT, puts it neatly near his, and puts the briefcase near KURT. BABETTE goes to SARA, takes a package from her, places it near the valise. Then she turns to BODO, takes the coats he is carrying, puts them neatly on top of the valises. After a second, KURT sits down. As he does so, we see that his movements are slow and careful, as if they are made with effort.)

BABETTE. (Points to a couch near which they are standing. She has a slight accent.) Is it allowed?
KURT. (SARA crosses L. Smiles. He has an accent.) Yes. It is allowed.

(KURT sits on couch S. L. BABETTE sits stiffly R. end of settee, motions to JOSHUA and BODO. BODO on her left. JOSHUA stands R. of settee.)

JOSHUA. (Nervously. He has a slight accent.) But we did not sound the bell ——
SARA. (Crosses R. Idly, as she wanders around room, her face excited.) The door isn't locked. It never was. Never since I can remember.
BODO. (Softly, puzzled.) The entrance of the home is never locked! So.

15

KURT. (*Looks at him.*) You find it curious to believe there are people who live and do not need to watch, eh, Bodo?

BODO. Yes, Papa.

KURT. (*Smiles.*) You and I.

JOSHUA. (*Smiles.*) It is strange. But it must be good, I think.

(SARA *to back of settee* R.)

KURT. Yes.

SARA. Sit back. Be comfortable. (*Calls softly.*) I wonder where Mama and David —— (*Delighted, sees portrait of* JOSHUA FARRELLY, *points to it.*) And that was my Father. (*Turns to them.*) That was the famous Joshua Farrelly. (*They all look up at it. She wanders around the room. Turns to* R. *look at room.*) My goodness, isn't it a fine room? I'd almost forgotten —— (*Turns to mantel* L.) And this was my grandmother. (*Giggles.*) An unpleasant woman with great opinions. (*Very nervously.* U. *to* L. *of* KURT.) Shall I go and say we're here? They'd be having breakfast, I think. Always on the side terrace in nice weather. I don't know. Maybe —— (*Up to piano. Picks up another picture from* D. *end of piano.*) "To Joshua and Fanny Farrelly. With admiration. Alfonso. May 7, 1910." (*Moves behind piano to keyboard upstage.*) I had an ermine boa and a pink coat. I was angry because it was too warm in Madrid to wear it.

BODO. Alfons von Spanien? Der hat immer Bilder von sich verschenkt. Ein Schlechtes Zeichen für einen Mann.

JOSHUA. (*Crosses* D. R. *to chair* D. R.) Mama told you it is good manners to speak the language of the country you visit. Therefore, speak in English.

BODO. (*Turns to* JOSHUA.) I said he seemed always to give his photograph. I said that is a bad flag on a man. Grow fat on the poor people and give pictures of the face.

(JOSHUA *sits* D. C.)

SARA. (*To* KURT.) I remember a big party and cakes and a glass of champagne for me. (*Crosses* R. *to* R. *of terrace door* R. *and looks at pictures on that wall.*) I was ten, I guess —— (*Suddenly laughs.*) That was when Mama said the first time a king got shot at he was a romantic, but the fifth time he was a comedian. And when Father gave his lecture in Madrid, he repeated it—right in Madrid. It was a great scandal. (*Turns to* CHILDREN.) You know, Alfonso was always getting shot at or bombed. (SARA

16

crosses to secretary, picks up small object, examines it and presses
it to her cheek.)

BODO. (Shrugs.) Certainement!

JOSHUA. Certainement? As-tu perdu la tete?

BABETTE. Speak in English, please.

KURT. (Without turning.) You are a terrorist, Bodo?

BODO. (Slowly.) No.

JOSHUA. Then since when has it become natural to shoot upon
people?

(SARA replaces small object in secretary.)

BODO. Do not give me lessons. It is neither right nor natural to
shoot upon people. I know that. (Leans to BABETTE.)

SARA. (To R. to U. R. table and places handbag on it. Looks at
BABETTE, thoughtfully.) An ermine boa. A boa is a scarf. I
should like to have one for you, Babbie. (Touches her hair.)
Once—(Crosses C. to U. R. of R. C. table—touching desk in pass-
ing.) in Prague, I saw a pretty one. I wanted to buy it for you.
But we had to pay our rent. (Laughs.) But I almost bought it.
(Crosses to C.)

BABETTE. Yes, Mama. Thank you. Fix your sash, Mama.

SARA. (Thoughtfully.) Almost twenty years. (Looks down at car-
pet. Laughs delightedly.)

BODO. You were born here, Mama?

SARA. Upstairs. And I lived here until I went to live with your
Father. (Looks out beyond terrace. U. C. to terrace step.) Your
Uncle David and I used to have a garden, behind the terrace. I
wonder if it's still there. I like a garden. I've always hoped we'd
have a house some day and settle down —— (Stops nervously,
turns to stare at KURT, who is looking at her. D. S. to table L. C.)
I am talking so foolish. Sentimental. At my age. Gardens and
ermine boas. I haven't wanted anything ——

KURT. (Comes toward her, takes her hand.) Sara, stop it. This is
a fine room. A fine place to be. Everything is so pleasant and full
of comfort; this will be a good piano on which to play again. And
it is all so clean. I like that. You shall not be a baby. You must
enjoy your house, and not be afraid that you hurt me with it.
Yes?

BABETTE. Papa, fix Mama's sash, please.

SARA. (Shyly smiles at him as KURT turns SARA around, ties sash.)

17

Yes, of course. It's strange, that's all. We've never been in a place like this together —— (*Turns to him.*)

KURT. That does not mean, and should not mean, that we do not remember how to enjoy what comes our way. We are on a holiday.

JOSHUA. A holiday? But for how long? And what plans for afterwards?

KURT. (*Crosses D. L. to L. end of sofa L. Quietly.*) We will have plans when the hour arrives to make them.

(SARA *is facing terrace.* ANISE *comes down stairs, stops, stares, amazed, a little frightened. She comes toward room, stares at children. The* MULLERS *have not seen her. As* SARA *turns,* ANISE *speaks.*)

ANISE. (*To above table D. R. Looking at* JOSHUA.) What? What?

(CHILDREN *rise.*)

SARA. (*Softly.*) Anise, it's me. It's Sara.

ANISE. (*Coming forward slowly. Then as she approaches* SARA, *she begins to run toward her.*) Miss Sara! Miss Sara! (*They reach each other, both laugh happily.* SARA *kisses* ANISE.) I would have known you. Yes, I would. I would have known. (*Excited, bewildered, nervous, looks toward* KURT. BODO *moves to R. of table R. C.* JOSHUA *comes to C. of desk behind sofa R.*) How do you do, sir? How do you do? (*Turns toward* CHILDREN.) How do you do? JOSHUA. Thank you, Miss Anise. We are in good health.

SARA. (*Happily.*) You look the same. I think you look the same. Just the way I've always remembered. (*To* OTHERS. *They step down a bit.* SARA *holds* ANISE *throughout this scene.*) This is the Anise I've told you about. She was here before I was born.

(JOSHUA *crosses to behind table R. C.*)

ANISE. But how—did you just come in? What a way to come home! And after all the plans we've made. But you were to come on the twelve o'clock train and Mr. David was to meet you ——

BABETTE. (*Steps L.*) The twelve o'clock train was most expensive. We could not have come with that train. We liked the train we came on. It was most luxurious.

ANISE. (*Very nervous, rattled.*) But Madame Fanny will have a fit. (*Turns to* SARA.) I will call her —— She will not be able to contain herself. (*Starts up.*)

18

SARA. (*Softly. Stopping* ANISE.) I wanted a few minutes. I am nervous about coming home, I guess.

BODO. (*Conversationally.*) You are French, Madame Anise?

ANISE. Yes. I am from the Bas Rhin. (*She moves front and just past* SARA, *and bobs her head idiotically at* KURT.) Sara's husband. That is nice. That is nice.

BODO. Yes, your accent is from the north. That is fine country. We were in hiding there once ——

(BABETTE *touches his shoulder to silence him.*)

ANISE. Hiding? You —— (*Turns nervously to* KURT.) But here we stand and talk. You have not had your breakfast, sir!

BABETTE. (*Simply.*) It would be nice to have breakfast.

ANISE. (*Crosses* SARA *to* C.) Yes, of course. I will go and order it.

SARA. (*To* CHILDREN.) What would you like for breakfast?

BABETTE. What would we like? Why, Mama, we will have anything that can be spared. If eggs are not too rare or too expensive ——

ANISE. (*Amazed.*) Expensive! Why—oh—I—I—must call Miss Fanny now. (*Crosses up to* C. *terrace door.*) It is of a necessity. Miss Fanny! Miss Fanny! (*Turns back to* SARA.) Have you forgotten your Mama's nature? She cannot bear not knowing things. Miss Fanny! What a way to come home. (BABETTE *sits* R. *end of sofa* R.) After twenty years. And nobody at the station.

FANNY'S VOICE. (*Off* R.) Don't yell at me. What is the matter with you?

ANISE. (*Excitedly, as* FANNY *draws near.*) She's here. They're here. Miss Sara. She's here, I tell you.

(FANNY *comes up to her, entering from* U. R. *Stops at step, stares at her, stares at* BODO *and* JOSHUA *on the floor, looks slowly around until she sees* SARA. ANISE U. R. *as* FANNY *enters.*)

SARA. (*Softly.*) Hello, Mama.

FANNY. (*After a long pause, softly, coming toward her.*) Sara. Sara, darling. You're here. (*Crosses down to* R. *of* SARA.) You're really here. (*She reaches her, takes her arms, kisses her, stares at her, smiles.*) Welcome. Welcome. Welcome to your house. (*After a second, looks at* SARA.) You're not young, Sara.

SARA. (*Smiles.*) No, Mama. I'm forty-one.

FANNY. (*Softly.*) Forty-one. Of course. (*Presses her arms again.*) Oh, Sara, I'm —— (*Then quickly.*) You look more like Papa now.

19

That's good. The years have helped you. (*Embraces her. Turns to look at* KURT.) Welcome to this house, sir.

KURT. (*Warmly.*) Thank you, Madame.

FANNY. (*Turns to look at* SARA *again, nervously pats her arm. Nods, turns again to stare at* KURT. *She is nervous and chatty. Crosses* D. L. *to* KURT.) You are a good-looking man, for a German. I didn't remember you that way. I like a good-looking man. (*Shakes his hand.*) I always have.

KURT. (*Smiles.*) I like a good-looking woman. I always have.

FANNY. Good. That's the way it should be.

BODO. (*From* R. *of table* R. C., *who is just rising from floor, to* SARA.) Ist das Grossmama? (*Crosses to* C.)

FANNY. (*Looks down.*) Yes. I am your grandmother. Also, I speak German, so do not talk about me. I speak languages very well. But there is no longer anybody to speak with. Anise has half-forgotten her French, which was always bad; and I have nobody with whom to speak my Italian or German or —— Oh, Sara— (SARA *down to* FANNY.) it's good to have you home. I'm chattering away, I ——

JOSHUA. Now you have us, Madame. We speak ignorantly, but fluently, in German, French, Italian, Spanish ——

KURT. And boastfully, in English.

JOSHUA. (*Softly.*) I am sorry, Papa. You have right.

BODO. (*To* JOSHUA.) There is never a need for boasting. If we are to fight for the good of all men, it is to be accepted that we must be among the most advanced. (*Crosses to below table* R. C.)

ANISE. (D. S. *a bit from* U. C.) My God.

FANNY. (*To* SARA.) Are these your *children?* Or are they dressed up midgets?

SARA. (*Laughs.*) These are my children, Mama. This, Babette. (BABETTE *bows.*) This, Joshua. (JOSHUA D. S. *two steps, bows.*) This is Bodo. (BODO *bows.*)

FANNY. (*Crosses to* JOSHUA.) Joshua was named for Papa. You wrote me. (*Kisses him. Indicates picture of* JOSHUA FARRELLY.) You bear a great name, young man.

JOSHUA. (*Smiles, indicates his father.*) My name is Muller.

FANNY. (*Looks at him, laughs.*) Yes. You look a little like your grandfather. (*To* BABETTE. *Crosses* R. *to* BABETTE, *above* BODO.) And so do you. You are a nice looking girl. (*To* BODO.) You look like nobody.

BODO. (*Proudly.*) I am not beautiful.

FANNY. (*Laughs.*) Well, Sara, well. (BABETTE *on* R. *end of sofa* R.) Three children. You have done well. (*To* KURT, *crosses* L. *to* KURT.) You, too, sir, of course. Are you quite recovered? Sara wrote that you were in Spain and ——

BODO. Did Mama write that Papa was a great hero? He was brave, he was calm, he was expert, he was resourceful, he was ——

KURT. (*Laughs.*) My biographer. And as unprejudiced as most of them.

SARA. (D. *to* R. *of* FANNY.) Where is David? I am so anxious —— Has he changed much? Does he ——

FANNY. (*To* ANISE.) Don't stand there. (*Crosses* U. *to* ANISE; SARA *moves* L. *to* R. *of* KURT.) Go and get him right away. (*Peers in the basket.*) Go get David. (JOSHUA *crosses up to door* U. R. *and looks out at terrace. As* ANISE *exits.*) He's out having breakfast with the titled folk. (D. S. *to* R. *of* SARA.) Do you remember Marthe Randolph? I mean, do you remember Hortie Randolph, her mother, who was my friend? Can you follow what I'm saying? I'm not speaking well today.

SARA. (*Laughs.*) Of course I remember Marthe and Hortie. You and she used to scream at each other.

(JOSHUA *leaves the window and goes to secretary* R., *picks up book.*)

FANNY. (*Takes* SARA'S *arm, brings her to settee, they sit,* FANNY R. *of* SARA.) Well, Marthe, her daughter, married Teck de Brancovis. Count de Brancovis. He was fancy when she married him. Not so fancy now, I suspect. Although still chic and tired. You know what I mean, the way they are in Europe. Well, they're here.——

(JOSHUA *looks at pages in book through this.*)

SARA. What's David like now? I ——

FANNY. Like? Like? I don't know. He's a lawyer. You know that. Papa's firm. He's never married. You know that, too ——

SARA. Why hasn't he married?

FANNY. Really, I don't know. I don't think he likes his own taste. Which is very discriminating of him. He's had a lot of girls, of course, one more ignorant and silly than the other —— (*Grins to* KURT. *Goes toward terrace, begins to scream.*) And where is he? David! David —— (*Goes* U. C. *to door,* BODO *follows her.*) ANISE'S VOICE. (*From* U. R.) He's coming, Miss Fanny. He's com-

21

ing. Contain yourself. He was down at the garage getting ready to leave ——

FANNY. I don't care where he is. Tell him to come. His sister comes home after twenty years —— David! I'm getting angry.

BODO. You must not get angry. We never do. Anger is protest. And so you must direction it to the proper channels and then harness it for the good of other men. That is correct, Papa?

FANNY. (*Crosses* R. *to* BODO. *Peers down at him.*) If you grow up to talk like that, and stay as ugly as you are, you are going to have one of those successful careers on the lecture platform.

(JOSHUA *and* BABETTE *laugh.*)

JOSHUA. Ah. It is a great pleasure to hear Grandma talk with you.

(KURT *has wandered to the piano. Standing, he touches the keys in the first bars of Mozart's Rondo in D Major.* DAVID *comes in from entrance hall* R. *At door, he stops and stares at* SARA. *Piano stops—*KURT *rises.*)

DAVID. (*To* SARA.) Sara. Darling ——

SARA. (*Wheels, goes running toward him. She moves into his arms. He leans down, kisses her with great affection.*) David. David. (*Crosses* R. *to* DAVID, *who has stopped above chair* L. *of table* D. R.)

(BABETTE *takes two steps* R. *to front of* L. *end of sofa.* JOSHUA *crosses to* L. *of table* R. C. KURT *crosses* D. *to* C.)

DAVID. (*Softly.*) It's been a long, long time. I got to thinking it would never happen. (*He leans down, kisses her hair. After a minute he smiles, presses her arm.*)

SARA. (*Excited.*) David, I'm excited. Isn't it strange? To be here, to see each other —— But I'm forgetting —— This is my husband and these are my children. Babette, Joshua, Bodo.

(JOSHUA D. L. *of* BODO, *who is* L. *of* BABETTE.)

ALL THREE. How do you do, Uncle David? (*The* BOYS *move forward to shake hands.* BODO, *followed by* JOSHUA, *crosses. They shake hands and go to stand* R. *of their mother.*)

DAVID. (*As he shakes hands with* JOSHUA.) Boys can shake hands. But so pretty a girl must be kissed. (*He kisses her. She smiles, very pleased.*)

22

BABETTE. Thank you. (*She crosses front to* R. *then to above* **SARA**.) Fix your hairpin, Mama.

(SARA *shoves back a falling pin.* DAVID *and* KURT *move to meet front of table* R. C. FANNY *sits* R. *end of sofa* L.)

DAVID. (*To* KURT.) I'm happy to meet you, sir, and to have you here.

KURT. Thank you. Sara has told me so much from you. You have a devoted sister.

(SARA *crosses to* DAVID'S R. *and takes his arm.* ANISE *sticks her head in from the hall.*)

ANISE. (*Enters from* R., *crosses to* C.) Your breakfast is coming. Shall I wash the children, Miss Sara?

JOSHUA. (D. R. *two steps. Amazed.*) Wash us? Do people wash each other?

SARA. No, but the washing is a good idea. (ANISE *crosses* R. *to door, turns.*) Go along now, and hurry. (*All* THREE *start for hall.*) And then we'll all have a fine big breakfast again.

(*The* CHILDREN *exit* R.)

FANNY. Again? Don't you usually have a good breakfast?

KURT. (*Smiles, sits* D. L.) No, Madame. Only sometimes.

SARA. (*Laughs.*) Oh, we do all right, usually. (*Sees* DAVID *staring at her, puts her hands in his affectionately. Very happily, very gaily.*) Ah, it's good to be here. We were kids. Now we're all grown up! I've got children, you're a lawyer, and a fine one, I bet ——

FANNY. The name of Farrelly on the door didn't, of course, hurt David's career.

DAVID. (*Smiles.*) Sara, you might as well know that Mama thinks of me only as a monument to Papa, and a not very well-made monument at that. I am not the man Papa was.

SARA. (*To* FANNY, *smiles.*) How do you know he's not?

FANNY. (*Carefully.*) I beg your pardon. That is the second time you have spoken disrespectfully of your father. (SARA *and* DAVID *laugh.* FANNY *turns to* KURT.) I hope you will like me.

KURT. I hope so.

SARA. (*Pulls him to couch, sits down with him.*) And I want to hear about you, David. (*Looks at him, laughs.*) I'm awfully nervous about seeing you. Are you about me?

23

DAVID. Yes, I certainly am.

SARA. (*Looks around.*) I'm like an idiot. I want to see everything right away. The lake, and my old room, and the nursery, and is the asparagus-bed where it used to be, and I want to talk and ask questions ——

KURT. (*Laughs.*) More slow, Sara. It is most difficult to have twenty years in a few minutes.

SARA. Yes, I know, but —— Oh, well. Kurt's right. We'll say it all slowly. It's just nice being back. Haven't I fine children?

DAVID. Very fine. You're lucky. I wish I had them.

FANNY. How could you have them? All the women you like are too draughty, if you know what I mean. I'm sure that girl from Lansing, Michigan, would be sterile. Which is as God in his wisdom would have it.

SARA. Oh. So you have a girl?

DAVID. I have no girl. This amuses Mama.

FANNY. (*To* KURT.) He's very attractive to some women. (*Points to* DAVID.) He's flirting with our Countess now, Sara. You will see for yourself.

DAVID. (*Sharply.*) You are making nervous jokes this morning, Mama. And they're not very good ones.

FANNY. (*Gaily.*) I tell the truth. If it turns out to be a joke, all the better.

SARA. (*Affectionately.*) Ah, Mama hasn't changed. And that's good, too.

FANNY. Don't mind me, Sara. I, too, am nervous about seeing you. (*To* KURT.) You'll like it here. You are an engineer?

KURT. Yes, Madame.

FANNY. Do you remember the day we met in Muenchen? The day Sara brought you to lunch? I thought you were rather a clod, and that Sara would have a miserable life. I think I was wrong. (*To* DAVID.) You see? I always admit when I'm wrong.

DAVID. You are a woman who is noble in all things, at all times.

FANNY. Oh, you're mad at me. (*To* KURT.) As I say, you'll like it here. I've already made some plans. The new wing will be for you and Sara. The old turkey-house we'll fix up for the children. A nice, new bathroom, and we'll put in their own kitchen, and Anise will move in with them ——

SARA. That's kind of you, Mama. But —— (*Very quietly.*) We won't make any plans for a while—a good, long vacation; God knows Kurt needs it ——

FANNY. (*To* SARA.) A vacation? (*To* KURT.) You'll be staying here, of course. You don't have to worry about work. . . . Engineers can always get jobs, David says, and he's already begun to inquire ——

KURT. I have not worked as an engineer since many years, Madame.

DAVID. Haven't you? I thought —— Didn't you work for Dornier?

KURT. Yes. Before '33.

FANNY. But you have worked in other places. A great many other places, I should say. Every letter of Sara's seemed to have a new postmark.

KURT. (*Smiles.*) We move most often.

DAVID. You·gave up engineering?

KURT. I gave it up? (*Smiles.*) Well, one could say it that way.

FANNY. What do you do?

SARA. Mama, we ——

KURT. It is difficult to explain.

DAVID. (*After a slight pause, a little stiffly.*) If you'd rather not . . .

FANNY. No. I—I'm trying to find out something. (*To* KURT.) May I ask it, sir?

KURT. Let me help you, Madame. You wish to know whether not being an engineer buys adequate breakfasts for my family. It does not. I have no wish to make a mystery of what I have been doing: it is only that it is awkward to place neatly. (*Smiles, motions with his hand.*) It sounds so big: it is so small. I am an anti-Fascist. And that does not pay well.

FANNY. Do you mind questions?

SARA. Yes.

KURT. (*Sharply.*) Sara. (*To* FANNY.) Perhaps I shall not answer them. But I shall try.

FANNY. Are you a radical?

KURT. You would have to tell me first what that word means to you, Madame.

FANNY. (*After a slight pause.*) That is just. Perhaps we all have private definitions. We all are anti-Fascists, for example ——

SARA. Yes. But Kurt works at it, Mama.

FANNY. What kind of work?

KURT. Any kind. Anywhere.

FANNY. (*Sharply.*) I will stop asking questions.

SARA. (*Very sharply.*) That would be sensible, Mama.

DAVID. Darling, don't be angry. We've been worried about you, naturally. We knew so little, except that you were having a bad time.

SARA. I didn't have a bad time. We never ——

KURT. Do not lie for me, Sara.

SARA. (*Rises.*) I'm not lying. (*Crosses to* C. *toward* FANNY.) I didn't have a bad time, the way they mean. I ——

FANNY. (*Slowly.* SARA *hesitates* C., *moves* U. C. *a few steps.*) You had a bad time just trying to live, didn't you? That's obvious, Sara, and foolish to pretend it isn't. Why wouldn't you take money from us? What kind of nonsense ——

SARA. (*Slowly to* FANNY.) We've lived the way we wanted to live. (*To* DAVID *and* FANNY.) I don't know the language of rooms like this any more. And I don't want to learn it again.

KURT. Do not bristle about it.

SARA. I'm not bristling. (*She moves toward* FANNY.) I married because I fell in love. You can understand that.

FANNY. (*Slowly.*) Yes.

SARA. (*Sits* R. *of* FANNY.) For almost twelve years Kurt went to work every morning and came home every night, and we lived modestly, and happily —— (*Sharply.*) As happily as people could in a starved Germany that was going to pieces ——

KURT. You're angry, Sara. Please. I do not like it that way. I will try to find a way to tell you with quickness. . . . Yes. (*To* FANNY *and* DAVID.) I was born in a town called Feurth. There is a holiday in my town. We call it Kirchweih. It was a gay holiday with games and music and a hot white sausage to eat with the wine. I grow up, I move away, to school, to work,—but always I come back for Kirchweih. For me, it is the great day of the year. (*Slowly.*) But, after the war, that day begins to change. The sausage is now made from bad stuff, the peasants come in without shoes, the children are now too sick —— (*Carefully.*) It is bad for my people, those years, but always I have hope. But in the festival of August, 1931, one year before the storm, I give up that hope. On that day I saw twenty-seven men murdered in a Nazi street fight. I say, I cannot just stand by now and watch. My time has come to move. (*Looks down, smiles.*) I say with Luther, " Here I stand. I can do nothing else. God help me. Amen."

SARA. It doesn't pay well to fight for what you believe in. But I wanted it, the way Kurt wanted it. (*Shrugs.*) They don't like us in

26

Europe: I guess they never did. So Kurt brought us home. You've always said you wanted us. If you don't, I will understand.

DAVID. Darling—of course we want you ——

FANNY. I am old. And made of dry cork. And bad-mannered. (*Rises, turns to* KURT.) Please forgive me.

SARA. (*Rises, goes quickly to* FANNY, *puts her hands on* FANNY'S *shoulders and turns her.*) Shut up, Mama. We're all acting like fools. I'm glad to be home. That's all I know. So damned glad.

(FANNY *kisses her.*)

DAVID. And we're damned glad to have you. So that's settled. (*Stretches his hand out to her. She comes to him.*) Come on. Let's walk to the lake. We've made it bigger and planted the island with blackberries. (*She smiles. Together they move out hall entrance.*)

FANNY. (*After a silence.*) They've always liked each other. (KURT D. S. *to* R. *of* FANNY.) We're going to have Zwetschgen-Knoedel for dinner. You like them?

KURT. Indeed.

FANNY. I hope you like decent food.

KURT. I do.

FANNY. That's a good sign in a man.

MARTHE. (*Coming in from terrace from* U. R. *Stops in doorway.*) Oh, I'm sorry, Fanny. We were waiting. (*Crosses* D. *to* C. R. *of mail table.*) I didn't want to interrupt the family reunion. I ——

FANNY. This is my son-in-law, Herr Muller. The Countess de Brancovis ——

KURT and MARTHE. (*Together.* KURT *crosses up to* L. *of* MARTHE.) How do you do?

MARTHE. And how is Sara, Mr. Muller? I haven't seen her since I was a little girl. She probably doesn't remember me at all. (TECK *comes in from hall. She turns.*) This is my husband, Herr Muller. (*Brings him down from door, crosses* R. *three steps.* TECK *at* R. *of* KURT.)

TECK. How do you do, sir? (KURT *bows. They shake hands.*) Would it be impertinent for one European to make welcome another?

KURT. (*Smiles.*) I do not think so. It would be friendly.

BODO. (*At door* R.) Papa! Oh! (MARTHE D. S. *to back of table.* TECK *follows, during speech. Sees* TECK *and* MARTHE, *bows,*

27

*crosses to* R. *of table* R. C.) Good morning. Miss Anise says you are the Count and Countess de Brancovis.

TECK. (*Laughs.*) How do you do?

(KURT *crosses to* R. *of sofa* L.)

MARTHE. (*Laughs.*) What's your name?

BODO. My name is Bodo. It's a strange name. No? (BODO *crosses to* KURT.) This is the house of great wonders. Each has his bed, each has his bathroom. The arrangement of it, that is splendorous.

FANNY. (*Laughs.*) You are a fancy talker, Bodo.

KURT. Oh, yes. In many languages.

BODO. (*To* FANNY.) Please to correct me when I am wrong. Papa, the plumbing is such as you have never seen. Each implement is placed on the floor, and all are simultaneous in the same room. (KURT *is amused.*) You will therefore see that being placed most solidly on the floor allows of no rats, rodents and crawlers, and is most sanitary. (*To* OTHERS.) Papa will be most interested. He likes to know how each thing of everything is put together. And he is so fond of being clean.

KURT. (*Laughs. To* FANNY.) I am a hero to my children. It bores everybody but me.

TECK. It is most interesting, Herr Muller. I thought I had a good ear for the accents of your country. But yours is most difficult to place. Yours is Bayerisch—or is it ——

BODO. That's because Papa has worked in so many . . .

KURT. (*Quickly placing hand on* BODO'S *shoulder and moving him up.*) German accents are the most difficult to identify. I, myself, when I try, am usually incorrect. It would be of a particular difficulty with me. I speak other languages. Yours would be Rumanian, would it not?

(BODO *to behind mail table.*)

MARTHE. (*Laughs.*) My God, is it that bad?

KURT. (*Smiles.*) I am showing off. I knew the Count de Brancovis is Rumanian.

TECK. (*Heartily.*) So? We have met before? I thought so, but I cannot remember ——

KURT. No, sir. We have not met before. I read your name in the newspapers.

TECK. (*To* KURT.) Strange. I was sure I had met you. I was in the

28

Paris Legation for many years, and I thought perhaps we met there ——

KURT. No. If it is possible to believe, I am the exile who is not famous. (*He turns to* FANNY.) I have been thinking with pleasure, Madame Fanny, of breakfast on your porch. (*Points to the portrait of* JOSHUA FARRELLY.) Your husband once wrote: " I am getting older and Europe seems far away. Fanny and I will have an early breakfast on the porch—(*Points to the terrace.*) and then I shall drive the bays into Washington." And then he goes on saying, " Henry Adams tells me he has been reading Karl Marx. I shall have to tell him my father made me read Marx many years ago, and that, since he proposes to exhibit himself to impress me, will spoil Henry's Sunday."

FANNY. (*Laughs delightedly. She rises, takes* KURT'S *arm.*) And so it did. I had forgotten that. I am pleased with you. I shall come and serve your food myself. I had forgotten Joshua ever wrote it.

(*They start out the terrace door together.*)

KURT. (*As they disappear.*) I try to impress you. I learned it last night. (*She laughs, they disappear.*)

TECK. (*Smiles.*) He is a clever man. A quotation from Joshua Farrelly. That is the sure road to Fanny's heart. (*He has turned to look at* KURT'S *valise.*) Where did you say Herr Muller came from?

MARTHE. Germany.

TECK. I know that. (*Has gone to table where valise has been placed, leans over, stares at it, pushes it, looks at labels, opens and closes lock.*) What part of Germany?

MARTHE. (*Taking cigarette and lighting it.*) I don't know. And I never knew you were an expert on accents.

TECK. (*Going to where* JOSHUA *has placed* KURT'S *briefcase.*) I never knew it either. Are you driving into Washington with David this morning?

MARTHE. (*Crosses to front of sofa* L.) I was going to. But he may not be going to the office, now that Sara's here. I was to have lunch with Sally Tyne. (*Sits* R. *end of sofa.* TECK *has picked up the briefcase and is trying the lock.*) What are you doing?

TECK. Wondering why luggage is unlocked, and a shabby briefcase is so carefully locked.

MARTHE. You're very curious about Herr Muller.

TECK. Yes. And I do not know why. Something far away —— I

29

am curious about a daughter of the Farrellys who marries a German who has bullet scars on his face and broken bones in his hands.

MARTHE. (*Sharply.*) Has he? There are many of them now, I guess.

TECK. (*Looks at her.*) So there are. But this one is in (*Crosses* D. L. *to bell pull.*) this house.

MARTHE. It is—is he any business of yours?

TECK. (*Pulls bell, then crosses to* U. C. *looking at luggage* R.) What is my business? Anything might be my business now.

MARTHE. Yes—unfortunately. (*Sharply as he presses the catch of valise, it opens, he closes it.*) You might inquire from your friend, Von Seitz. They always know their nationals.

TECK. (*Pleasantly, ignoring the sharpness with which she has spoken.*) Oh, yes, I will do that, of course. But I do not like to ask questions without knowing the value of the answers.

MARTHE. (*Rises, crosses to* TECK.) This man is a little German Sara married years ago. I remember Mama talking about it. He was nothing then, and he isn't now. They've had a tough enough time already without . . .

TECK. Have you —— Have you been sleeping with David?

MARTHE. (*Stops, stares at him, then simply.*) No. I have not been. (*Turns away, crosses* L. *and puts out cigarette in ashtray on mail table.*) And that hasn't been your business for a good many years now.

TECK. You like him?

MARTHE. (*Nervously. Steps toward* TECK.) What's this for, Teck?

TECK. Answer me, please.

MARTHE. I —— (*She stops.*)

TECK. Yes? Answer me.

MARTHE. I do like him.

TECK. What does he feel about you?

MARTHE. I don't know.

(*There is a pause.*)

TECK. But you are trying to find out. You have made any plans with him?

MARTHE. Of course not. I ——

TECK. But you will try to make him have plans. I have recognized it. Well, we have been together a long time. (JOSEPH *enters* L.

TECK *stops, crosses to* R. *end of sofa* L.) Joseph, Miss Fanny wishes you to take the baggage upstairs.

JOSEPH. (*Crosses* R. *to baggage.*) Yes, sir. I was going to. (*He begins to pick up baggage.*)

(MARTHE *has turned sharply and is staring at* TECK. *Then she rises, crosses to back of chair* R. C., *watches* JOSEPH *pick up baggage, turns again to look at* TECK.)

TECK. As I was saying. It is perhaps best that we had this talk.

MARTHE. I —— (*She stops, waits for* JOSEPH *to move off. He exits, carrying valises.*) Why did you do that? Why did you tell Joseph that Fanny wanted him to take the baggage upstairs?

TECK. (*Has risen.*) Obviously, it is more comfortable to look at baggage behind closed doors. (*Crosses her, continuing to door* R.)

MARTHE. (*Very sharply.*) What kind of silliness is this now? (*Crosses* R., *grabs his arm and turns him. They are behind table* D. R.) Leave these people alone —— (*As he starts to exit.*) I won't let you ——

TECK. What? (*As he moves again, she comes after him.*)

MARTHE. I said, I won't let you. You are not ——

TECK. (*Grabs her wrist and twists it.*) How many times have you seen me angry? (MARTHE *looks up, startled.*) You will not wish to see another. (*Releases her wrist.*) Run along now and have lunch with something you call Sally Tyne. But do not make plans with David. You will not be able to carry them out. You will go with me, when I am ready to go. You understand. (*He exits during his speech. The last words come as he goes through door, and as . . .*)

## THE CURTAIN FALLS

31

# ACT II

SCENE: *The same as Act I, eight days later. It is beginning to grow dark, the evening is warm, and the terrace
doors are open.*

AT RISE: SARA *is sitting on couch, crocheting.* FANNY
*and* TECK *are sitting at a small table playing cribbage.*
BODO *is sitting near them, at a large table, working on a
heating pad. The cord is torn from the bag, the bag is
ripped open.* ANISE *sits next to him anxiously watching
him. Outside on the terrace,* JOSHUA *is going through
baseball motions, coached by* JOSEPH. *From time to
time, they move out of sight, reappear, move off again.*

FANNY. (*Playing a card.*) One.

BODO. (*Pulling wires from heating pad. To* ANISE, *then to* TECK.)
The arrangement of this heating pad grows more complex.

TECK. (*Smiles, moves on cribbage board.*) And the more wires you
remove, the more complex it will grow.

BODO. (*Points to bag.*) Man has learned to make man comfortable.
Yet all cannot have the comforts. (*To* ANISE.) How much did this
cost you?

ANISE. It cost me ten dollars. And you have made a ruin of it.

BODO. That is not yet completely true. (*Turns to* FANNY.) Did I
not install for you a twenty-five cent button-push for your radio?

FANNY. Yes, you're quite an installer.

TECK. (*Playing a card.*) Two and two.

BODO. (*To* TECK.) As I was wishing to tell you, Count de Brancovis, comfort and plenty exist. Yet all cannot have it. Why?

TECK. I do not know. It has worried many men. Why?

ANISE. (*To* BODO.) Yes—why?

BODO. (*Takes a deep breath, raises his finger as if about to lecture.*) Why? (*Considers a moment, then deflates himself.*) I am
not as yet sure.

ANISE. I thought not.

FANNY. (*Calling. Turns to look at* JOSHUA *and* JOSEPH *on terrace.*) Would you mind doing that dancing some place else?

32

JOSEPH. (*Looking in.*) Yes'm. That ain't dancing. I'm teaching Josh baseball.

FANNY. Then maybe he'd teach you how to clean the silver.

JOSEPH. (*Crosses down to above table* C. JOSHUA *stands in door* U. C.) I'm a good silver-cleaner, Miss Fanny.

FANNY. But you're getting out of practice.

JOSEPH. (*After a moment's thought.*) Yes'm. I see what you mean. (*He exits* L.)

FANNY. (*Playing a card.*) Three.

JOSHUA. (*Crosses* D. *to* U. C., *tossing ball and catching it.*) It is my fault. I'm crazy about baseball.

BODO. Baseball players are among the most exploited people in this country. I read about it. . . .

FANNY. You never should have learned to read.

BODO. (JOSHUA *crosses* R. *to* BODO, *moving above sofa* R.) Their exploited condition is foundationed on the fact that ——

JOSHUA. (*Bored.*) All right, all right. I still like baseball. (*He turns back to* U. C., *but stops and turns at* FANNY'S VOICE.)

TECK. (*Playing a card.*) Five and three.

SARA. Founded, Bodo, not foundationed.

JOSHUA. (*Crosses* U. R. *of table above sofa* R.) He does it always. He likes long words. In all languages.

TECK. How many languages do you children speak?

BODO. Oh, we do not really know any very well, except German and English. We speak bad French and ——

SARA. And bad Danish and bad Czech.

TECK. (*Turns to* SARA.) You seem to have stayed close to the borders of Germany. Did Herr Muller have hopes, as so many did, that National Socialism would be overthrown on every tomorrow?

(JOSHUA *crosses behind sofa to above table* C.)

SARA. We have not given up that hope. Have you, Count de Brancovis?

TECK. (*Turns back to game.*) I never had it.

JOSHUA. (*Pleasantly.*) Then it must be most difficult for you to sleep.

TECK. I beg your pardon?

(JOSHUA *starts to reply.*)

SARA. Schweig doch, Joshua!

FANNY. (*To* TECK.) Sara told Joshua to shut up. (*Playing card.*) Twelve.

TECK. I have offended you, Mrs. Muller. I am most sorry.

SARA. (*Pleasantly.*) No, sir, you haven't offended me. I just don't like polite political conversations any more.

TECK. (*Nods.*) All of us, in Europe, had too many of them.

SARA. Yes. Too much talk. By this time all of us must know where we are, and what we have to do. (TECK *turns back to game.*) It's an indulgence to sit in a room and discuss your beliefs as if they were a juicy piece of gossip.

FANNY. (JOSHUA *comes* D. *to behind table* C.) You know, Sara, I find it very pleasant that Kurt, considering his background, doesn't make platform speeches. He hasn't tried to convince anybody of anything.

SARA. (*Smiles.*) Why should he, Mama? You are quite old enough to have your own convictions—or Papa's.

FANNY. (*Turns to look at her.*) I am proud to have Papa's convictions.

SARA. Of course. But it might be well to have a few new ones, now and then.

FANNY. (*Peers over her.*) Are you criticizing me?

SARA. (*Smiles.*) Certainly not.

TECK. (*To* JOSHUA, *who is looking down at cribbage game.*) I didn't know your Father was a politician.

(BABETTE *enters* L., *runs to behind table* C., *carrying a plate and fork. She pushes* JOSHUA *out of his way to* R.)

JOSHUA. (*Looks at him for a second, then pleasantly.*) He wasn't, Count de Brancovis.

BABETTE. (*She has on an apron and she is carrying a plate. She goes to* FANNY.) Eat it while it's hot, Grandma.

(BODO *rises and quickly goes to* FANNY'S R. ANISE *follows and stands behind* BODO. FANNY *peers down, takes fork, begins to eat.* ANISE *and* BODO *both rise, move to* FANNY, *inspect the plate.*)

FANNY. (*To them.*) Go away.

ANISE. It is a potato pancake. (*Crosses back to behind table* R. *and looks at dismantled heating pad.*)

FANNY. (*Irritably.*) And it's the first good one I've eaten in many, many years. I love a good potato pancake.

34

BODO. (*Moving closer to* FANNY.) I, likewise.

(FANNY *nudges him away with her elbow.*)

BABETTE. I am making a great number for dinner.
TECK. (*Playing a card.*) Fifteen and two.
BABETTE. Move away, Bodo.

(BODO *goes to* R. *behind table* R.)

ANISE. (*As* BODO *comes to her.*) You have ruined it! I shall sue you. (*She sits in chair* R. *of table* R.)
JOSHUA. I told you not to let him touch it.
SARA. (*Laughs.*) I remember you were always saying that, Anise— that you were going to sue. That's very French. I was sick once in Paris, and Babbie (BABETTE *crosses to chair* U. R. C. *taking off apron. She takes sewing material and sewing basket from bag on chair, leaving apron there.*) finished a dress I was making for a woman on the Rue Jacob. The woman admitted the dress was well done, but said she was going to sue because I hadn't done it all. Fancy that.

(BABETTE *crosses* R. *around sofa* R. *and sits beside* FANNY *and sews.*)

FANNY. (*Slowly.*) You sewed for a living?
SARA. Not a very good one. But Babbie and I made a little something now and then. Didn't we, darling?
FANNY. (*Sharply.*) Really, Sara, were these—these things necessary, Sara? Why couldn't you have written?
SARA. (*Laughs.*) Mama, you've asked me that a hundred times in the last week.
JOSHUA. (*Gently.*) I think it is only that Grandma feels sorry for us. Grandma has not seen much of the world.
FANNY. Now, don't you start giving me lectures, Joshua. I'm fond of you. And of you too, Babbie. (*To* ANISE.) Are there two desserts for dinner? And are they sweet?
ANISE. Yes.
FANNY. (*Turns to* BODO.) I wish I were fond of you.
BODO. You are. (*Happily.*) You are very fond of me.
FANNY. (*Playing a card.*) Twenty-five.
TECK. (*Playing last card.*) Twenty-eight and one.

(JOSHUA *goes to secretary to get a book. He crosses to chair* U. C., *examines light from window, sits, and reads.*)

FANNY. (*Counting score.*) A sequence and three, a pair and five. (*To* TECK, *as they finish cribbage game.*) There. That's two dollars off. I owe you eighty-fifty.

(BODO *sits* L. *of table* R.)

TECK. Let us carry it until tomorrow. You shall give it to me as a going-away token.

FANNY. (*Too pleased.*) You're going away?

TECK. (*Laughs.*) Ah, Madame Fanny. Do not sound *that* happy.

FANNY. Did I? That's rude of me. When are you going?

TECK. In a few days, I think. (*Turns to look at* SARA.) We're too many refugees, eh, Mrs. Muller?

SARA. (*Pleasantly.*) Perhaps.

TECK. Will you be leaving, also?

SARA. I beg your pardon.

TECK. I thought perhaps you, too, would be moving on. Herr Muller does not give me the feeling of a man who settles down. Men who have done his work seldom leave it. Not for a quiet country house.

(*All three* CHILDREN *look up.*)

SARA. (*Very quietly.*) What work do you think my husband has done, Count de Brancovis?

TECK. Engineering?

SARA. (*Slowly, nods.*) Yes. Engineering.

FANNY. (*Very deliberately to* TECK. JOSHUA *back to book,* BABETTE *to sewing.*) I don't know what you're saying. They shall certainly not be leaving—ever. Is that understood, Sara?

SARA. Well, Mama ——

FANNY. There are no wells about it. You've come home to see me *die* and you will wait until I'm ready.

(CHILDREN *look at* FANNY.)

SARA. (*Laughs.*) Really, Mama, that isn't the reason I came home.

FANNY. It's a good enough reason. I shall do a fine death. I intend to be a great deal of trouble to everybody.

(CHILDREN *smile and go back to what they were doing.*)

ANISE. I daresay.

FANNY. I shall take to my bed early, and stay for years. In great pain.

ANISE. I am sure of it. You will duplicate the disgrace of the birth of Miss Sara.

SARA. (*Laughs.*) Was I born in disgrace?

ANISE. (FANNY *becomes interested in* BABETTE'S *work.*) It was not your fault. But it was disgusting. Three weeks before you were to come—all was excellent, of course, in so healthy a woman as Madame Fanny—a great dinner was given here, and, most unexpectedly, attended by a beautiful lady from England.

FANNY. Do be still. You are dull and fanciful ——

ANISE. Mr. Joshua made the great error of waltzing the beauty for two dances, Madame Fanny being unfitted for the waltz, and under no circumstances being the most graceful of dancers.

FANNY. (*Her voice rising.*) Are you crazy? I danced magnificently. I ——

ANISE. It is well you thought so. A minute did not elapse between the second of the waltzes, and a scream from Madame Fanny. She was in labor. (FANNY *turns to table and puts cards in box.*) Two hundred people, and if we had left her alone, she would have remained in the ballroom ——

FANNY. How you invent! How you invent!

ANISE. Do not call to me that I am a liar. For three weeks you are in the utmost agony ——

FANNY. And so I was. I remember it to this day ——

ANISE. (*To* SARAH, *angrily.* FANNY *continues to straighten table.*) Not a pain. Not a single pain. She would lie up there in state, stealing candy from herself. Then, when your Papa would rest himself for a minute at the dinner or with a book, a scream would dismantle the house—it was revolting. (*Spitefully to* FANNY.) And now, the years have passed, and I may disclose to you that Mr. Joshua knew you were going through the play-acting ——

FANNY. (*Rises.*) He did not. You are a malicious, miserable ——

ANISE. Once he said to me, "Anise, it is well that I am in love. This is of a great strain, and her great-uncle Freddie was not right in the head, neither."

FANNY. (*Rises. Screaming.*) You will leave this house —— You are a liar, (ANISE *rises.*) a thief, a woman of ——

SARA. Mama, sit down.

ANISE. (*Moves below table toward* FANNY.) I will certainly leave this house. I will —— (*Picks up wool she has dropped at her feet.*)

37

SARA. (*Sharply.*) Both of you. Sit down. And be still.

ANISE. She has intimated that I lie ——

FANNY. (*Screaming.*) Intimate! Is that what I was doing —— (ANISE *begins to leave the room.*) Very well! I beg your pardon. I apologize.

(ANISE *turns.*)

SARA. Both of you. You are acting like children.

BODO. Really, Mama. You insult us.

ANISE. (*Crosses to chair* R. *of table* D. R.) I accept your apology. Seat yourself.

(*They both sit down at same time.*)

FANNY. (*After a silence.*) I am unloved.

BABETTE. I love you, Grandma.

FANNY. Do you, Babbie?

JOSHUA. And I.

FANNY. (*Nods, very pleased. To* BODO.) And you?

BODO. I loved you the primary second I saw you.

FANNY. You are a charlatan.

ANISE. As for me, I am fond of all the living creatures. It is true, the children cause me greater work, which in turn more greatly inconveniences my feet, however I do not complain. I believe in children.

FANNY. Rather like believing in the weather, isn't it? (DAVID *and* KURT *come in from terrace. Both are in work clothes, their sleeves rolled up.* DAVID *enters door* U. L., *crosses to secretary to fill pipe there.*) Where have you been?

DAVID. We've been helping Mr. Chabeuf spray the fruit trees.

ANISE. Mr. Chabeuf says that Herr Muller has the makings of a good farmer. From a Frenchman that is a large thing to say.

KURT. (*Rolling down sleeves, putting on coat as he comes* D. C. *He has looked around room, looked at* TECK, *strolled over to* BODO.) Mr. Chabeuf and I have an excellent time exchanging misinformation. (*To* TECK, *in passing.*) My father was a farmer. I have a wide knowledge of farmers' misinformation.

FANNY. This is good farm land. Perhaps, in time ——

(DAVID *crosses to back of* TECK'S *chair.*)

DAVID. (*Laughs.*) Mama would give you the place, Kurt, if you guaranteed that your great-grandchildren would die here.

KURT. (*At behind table* D. R.—*Smiles.*) I would like to so guarantee.

TECK. A farmer. That is very interesting. Abandon your ideals, Mr. Muller?

KURT. Ideals? (*Carefully.*) Sara, heist es auf Deutsch " Ideale " ?

SARA. Yes.

KURT. Is that what I have now? I do not like the word. It gives to me the picture of a small, pale man at a seaside resort. (*To* BODO.) What are you doing?

BODO. Preparing an elderly electric pad for Miss Anise. I am confused.

KURT. (*Wanders toward piano.*) So it seems.

BODO. Something has gone wrong with the principle on which I have been working. It is probable that I will ask your assistance.

KURT. (*Bows to him, standing behind keyboard.*) Thank you. (*Begins to pick out notes with one hand.*) Whenever you are ready! (KURT *sits at piano and plays Haydn Minuet in A Major— six bars and a chord ending.*)

FANNY. We shall have a little concert tomorrow evening. In honor of Babbie's birthday. (*To* KURT.) Kurt, you and I will play the Clock Symphony. Then Joshua and I will play the duet we've learned, and Babbie will sing. And I shall finish with a Chopin Nocturne.

DAVID. (*Laughs.*) I thought you'd be the last on the program.

(*Piano stops.* DAVID *crosses behind sofa toward* R.)

TECK. Where is Marthe?

FANNY. She'll be back soon. She went into town to do an errand for me. (*To* DAVID.) Did you buy presents for everybody?

DAVID. I did. (DAVID *comes* D. *to behind table* D. R.)

SARA. (*Smiles, to* BABETTE.) We always did that here. If somebody had a birthday, we all got presents. (KURT *plays again with one hand, improvisation.*) Nice, isn't it?

DAVID. (*To* ANISE—*looks closely at pad* BODO *is " repairing."*) I shall buy you an electric pad. You will need it.

ANISE. Indeed.

FANNY. Did you buy me a good present?

DAVID. Pretty good. (*Crosses to behind* R. *end of sofa* R. *Pats* BABETTE'S *head.*) The best present goes to Babbie: it's her birthday.

FANNY. Jewelry?

DAVID. No, not jewelry.

FANNY. Oh. Not jewelry.

DAVID. Why? Why should you want jewelry? You've got too many bangles now.

FANNY. I didn't say I wanted it. I just asked you.

TECK. (*Gets up.*) It was a natural mistake, David. You see, Mrs. Mellie Sewell told your mother that she had seen you and Marthe in Barstow's. And your mother said you were probably buying her a present, or one for Babbie.

DAVID. (*Too sharply.*) Yes.

TECK. (*Laughs.*) Yes what?

DAVID. (*Slowly.*) Just yes. (DAVID *crosses* U. *to window* U. R. C.)

FANNY. (*Too hurriedly.*) Mellie gets everything wrong. She's very anxious to meet Marthe because she used to know Francis Cabot, her aunt. Marthe's aunt, I mean, not Mellie's.

SARA. (*Too hurriedly.*) She really came to inspect Kurt and me. (KURT *plays irregularly and abstractedly, listening to conversation.*) But I saw her first. (*She looks anxiously at* DAVID *who has turned his back on the room and is facing the terrace.*) You were lucky to be out, David.

(DAVID *crosses to beside table* U. L. C.)

DAVID. Oh, she calls every Saturday afternoon, to bring Mama all the Washington gossip of the preceding week. She gets it all wrong, you understand, but that doesn't make any difference to either Mama or her. Mama then augments it, wits it up, Papa used to say ——

FANNY. Certainly. I sharpen it a little. Mellie has no sense of humor.

DAVID. So Mama sharpens it a little, and delivers it tomorrow afternoon to old lady Marcy down the road. Old lady Marcy hasn't heard a word in ten years, so she unsharpens it again, and changes the names. By Wednesday afternoon ——

TECK. (*Smiles. Turns in chair and interrupts* DAVID.) By Wednesday afternoon (KURT *stops playing.*) it will not be you who (DAVID *crosses* D. C. *to be on level with* TECK.) were in Barstow's, and it will be a large diamond pin with four sapphires delivered to Gaby Delys.

DAVID. (*Looks at him.*) Exactly.

FANNY. (*Very nervously.*) Francis Cabot is (DAVID *crosses in front of sofa* L. *and* U. L. *to* D. *end of piano.*) Marthe's aunt, you un-

40

derstand —— (*To* KURT.) Kurt, did you ever know Paul von Seitz, a German?

KURT. I have heard of him.

FANNY. (*Speaking very rapidly.*) Certainly. He was your Ambassador to somewhere. I've forgotten. Well, Francie Cabot married him. I could have. Any American, not crippled, whose father had money . . . He was crazy about me. I was better looking than Francie. Well, years later when he was your Ambassador— my father was, too, as you probably know—not your Ambassador, of course, ours—but I am talking about Von Seitz.

DAVID. (*Laughs to* KURT.) You can understand how it goes. Old lady Marcy is not entirely to blame.

(KURT *plays Mozart Minuet in B Flat Major with one hand.*)

FANNY. Somebody asked me if I didn't regret not marrying him. I said, " Madame, je le regrette tous les jours et j'en suis heureuse chaque soir." (FANNY *turns to* DAVID. TECK *turns to look at* KURT *at piano.*) That means I regret it every day and am happy about it every night. You understand what I meant, by *night?* Styles in wit change so.

DAVID. I understood it, Mama.

JOSHUA. We, too, Grandma.

BABETTE. (*Approvingly.*) It is most witty.

BODO. I do not know that I understood. You will explain to me, Grandma?

SARA. Later.

(KURT *continues to play, now both hands.*)

FANNY. (*Turns to look at* TECK.) You remember the old Paul von Seitz?

TECK. (*Turns to* FANNY. *Nods.*) He was stationed in Paris when I first was there.

FANNY. Of course. I always forget you were a diplomat.

TECK. It is just as well.

FANNY. There's something insane about a Roumanian diplomat. Pure insane. (TECK *turns back to* KURT.) I knew another one, once. At least he said he was a Roumanian. He wanted to marry me, too.

SARA. (*Laughs.*) All of Europe.

FANNY. Not all. Some. Naturally. I was rich, I was witty, my family was of the best. I was handsome, unaffected ——

DAVID. And noble and virtuous and kind and elegant and fashionable and simple—it's hard to remember everything you were. I've often thought it must have been boring for Papa to have owned such perfection.

FANNY. (*Shrieks.*) What! Your father bored with me! Not for a second of our life ——

DAVID. (*Laughs. Crosses D. to front of sofa L. and sits L. of* SARA.) Oh God, when will I learn?

BODO. Do not shriek, Grandma. It is an unpleasant sound for the ear.

(JOSHUA *rises, crosses to secretary, takes another book, stands there reading and listening.*)

SARA. Why, Mama! A defect in you has been discovered.

FANNY. Where was I? Oh, yes. What I started out to say was ——
(*She turns, carefully to* TECK.) Mellie Sewell told me, when you left the room, that she had heard from Louis Chandler's child's governess that you had won quite a bit of money in a poker game with Sam Chandler and some Germans at the Embassy and ——
(KURT *stops playing sharply, hitting a discord as his hands fall on keys.* TECK *turns to look at him.*) And that's how I thought of Von Seitz. His nephew Philip was in on the game.

DAVID. (*Looks at* TECK, *leans forward, elbow on knees.*) It must have been a big game. Sam Chandler plays in big games.

TECK. Not big enough.

DAVID. Have you known Sam long?

TECK. For years. (*Looks at* KURT.) Every Embassy in Europe knew him.

DAVID. (*Sharply.*) Sam and Nazis must make an unpleasant poker game.

(KURT *starts to play piano. Soldiers' Song.*)

TECK. (*Who has not looked away from* KURT.) I do not play poker to be amused.

DAVID. (*Irritably.*) What's Sam selling now?

TECK. Bootleg munitions. He always has.

DAVID. You don't mind?

TECK. Mind? I have not thought about it.

(BODO *puts heating pad cover behind him, testing its size against his back.*)

42

FANNY. Well, you ought to think about it. Sam Chandler has always been a scoundrel. All the Chandlers are. They're cousins (BODO *rises and crosses to behind* ANISE *and tests cover against her back.*) of mine. Mama used to say they never should have learned to walk on two feet. (TECK *turns in chair to look at* KURT. BABETTE *starts to hum song* KURT *plays;* JOSHUA *joins in.*) They would have been more comfortable on four.

TECK. (*To* KURT, *who has started to play again.*) Do you know the young Von Seitz, Herr Muller? He was your military attaché in Spain.

KURT. He was the German government attaché in Spain. I know his name, of course. He is a famous artillery expert. But the side on which I fought was not where he was stationed, Count de Brancovis.

ANISE. (BODO *has come around in back of her, and is trying to fit electric pad to her back.* BABETTE *and* JOSHUA *begin to hum song* KURT *is playing.* SARA *begins to hum.*) It is time for the bath and the change of clothes. I will give you five more minutes ——

(BODO *returns to his chair* L. *of table* D. R.)

FANNY. What is the song?

TECK. It was a German soldiers' song. They sang it as they straggled back in '18. I remember hearing it in Berlin. Were you there then, Herr Muller?

KURT. (*The playing and singing continue.*) I was not in Berlin.

TECK. (*Rises, crosses* U. *to* R. *of* KURT.) But you were in the war, of course?

KURT. Yes. I was in the war.

FANNY. You didn't think then you'd live to see another war.

KURT. Many of us were afraid we would.

FANNY. What are the words?

SARA. The Germans in Spain, in Kurt's Brigade, wrote new words for it.

(*Humming stops.*)

KURT. This is the way you heard it in Berlin in 1918. (*Begins to sing in German.*)

> " Wir zieh'n Heim, wir zieh'n Heim,
> Mancher kommt nicht mit,
> Mancher ging verschütt,
> Aber freunde sind wir stets."

*(In English.)*

"We come home. We come home.
Some of us are gone, and some of us are lost, but we
   are friends:
Our blood is on the earth together.
Some day. Some day we shall meet again.
Farewell."

*(Stops singing.)* At a quarter to six on the morning of November 7th, 1936, eighteen years later, five hundred Germans walked through the Madrid streets on their way to defend the Manzanares River. We felt good that morning. You know how it is to be good when it is needed to be good? So we had need of new words to say that. I translate with awkwardness, you understand. *(Begins to sing again in English.)*

"And so we have met again.
The blood on the earth did not have time to dry.
We lived to stand and fight again.
This time we fight for people.
This time the bastards—
Will keep their hands away.
Those who sell the blood of other men, this time,
They keep their hands away.
For us to stand.
For us to fight.
This time, no farewell, no farewell."

*(Music dies out. There is silence for a minute. Then* KURT *looks up.)* We did not win. *(Looks up, gently.)* It would have been a different world if we had.

SARA. Papa said so years ago. Do you remember, Mama? "For every man who lives without freedom, the rest of us must face the guilt."

*(*KURT *leans on piano, head in hand.)*

FANNY. "Yes, we are liable in the conscience-balance for the tailor in Lodz, the black man in our South, the peasant in ——" *(Turns to* TECK. *Unpleasantly.)* Your country, I think.

*(*TECK *crosses* D. *a step, smiling at* FANNY.)*

ANISE. *(Rises.)* Come. Baths for everybody. *(To* BODO.) Gather the wires. You have wrecked my cure.

(KURT *turns on stool to window.*)

BODO. If you would allow me a few minutes more ——

ANISE. (*Crosses to door* R., *stands above it.*) Come along. I have been duped for long enough. Come, Joshua. Babette. Baths.

JOSHUA. (*He takes book with him. Rises, crosses front to door, exits up stairs. Starts out after* ANISE. BABETTE *begins to gather up her sewing.*) My tub is a thing of glory. But I do not like it so prepared for me and so announced by Miss Anise. (*He exits. As he passes* BABETTE *rises, crosses* L. *and* U. *to chair* U. R. C., *leaves sewing material there.*)

BODO. (*Who has gathered his tools and heating pad, standing above table* R. *To* ANISE.) You are angry about this. I do not blame you with my heart or my head. I admit I have failed. But Papa will repair it, Anise. Will you not, Papa? (TECK *crosses to* BODO.) In a few minutes ——

TECK. (*To* BODO.) Your father is an expert electrician?

BODO. Oh, yes, sir.

TECK. And as good with radio ——

(BODO *begins to nod.*)

KURT. (*Rises. Sharply.*) Count de Brancovis, make your questions to me, please. Not to my children.

(OTHERS *look up, surprised.*)

TECK. (*Pleasantly, crosses front to* L. *in front of fireplace and sits in armchair.*) Very well, Mr. Muller.

ANISE. (*As she exits with* BODO.) Nobody can fix it. You have made a pudding of it.

BODO. (*As he follows her.*) Do not worry. In five minutes tonight you will have a pad far better —— (*As* BODO *reaches door, he bumps into* MARTHE *who is carrying a large dress box.*) Oh. Your pardon. Oh, hello. (*He disappears.*)

MARTHE. (*Gaily.*) Hello. (*To* FANNY.) I waited for them. I was afraid they wouldn't deliver this late in the day. (*To* SARA.) Come on, Sara. I can't wait to see them.

SARA. What?

MARTHE. (*Standing just on* R.) Dresses. From Fanny. A tan linen, and a dark green with wonderful buttons, a white *net* for Babbie, (BABETTE *crosses to back of* R. *end of sofa* R.) *and* a suit for you, and play dresses for Babbie, and a dinner dress in gray to wear for Babbie's birthday—gray should be good for you,

45

Sara—(SARA *rises*.) all from Savitt's. We sneaked the measurements, Anise and I ——

SARA. (*Crosses to above table* C. *to* FANNY.) How nice of you, Mama. How very kind of you. And of you, Marthe, to take so much trouble —— (KURT *comes to* R. *end of piano*. SARA *goes toward* FANNY. *She leans down, kisses* FANNY.) You're a sweet woman, Mama.

DAVID. (*Crosses to* MARTHE.) That's the first time Mama's heard that word. (*He takes boxes from* MARTHE, *puts them on table near door*. MARTHE *smiles at him and touches his hand as* TECK *watches them*.)

FANNY. (*As* DAVID *is crossing*.) I have a bottom sweetness, if you understand what I mean.

DAVID. I've been too close to the bottom to see it.

FANNY. That should be witty. I don't know why it isn't.

(BABETTE *comes over to stare at boxes*. DAVID *opens boxes and lets* BABETTE *peek during next speeches*.)

SARA. (*To* FANNY.) From Savitt's. Extravagant of you. They had such lovely clothes. I remember my coming out dress. (*She goes to* KURT.) Do you remember the black suit, with the braid, the first day we met? Well, that was from Savitt's. (*She is close to him*.) Me, in an evening dress. Now, you'll have to take me into Washington. I want to show off. (*She caresses his shoulder not looking at him. He looks to* TECK.) Next week, and we'll dance, maybe —— (*Sees he is not looking at her*.) What's the matter, darling? (*No answer. Slowly he turns to look at her*.) What's the matter, Kurt? Is it bad for me to talk like this? What have I done? It isn't that dresses have ever mattered to me, it's just that ——

KURT. Of course they have mattered to you. As they should. I do not think of the dress. (*Draws her to him*.) How many years have I loved that face?

SARA. (*Her face is very happy*.) So?

KURT. So. (*He leans down, kisses her, as if it were important*.)

SARA. (*Pleased, unembarrassed*.) There are other people here.

MARTHE. (*Slowly*.) And good for us to see.

TECK. Nostalgia?

MARTHE. No. Nostalgia is for something you have known.

(FANNY *coughs*.)

46

BABETTE. (*Comes to* FANNY.) Grandma—it is allowed to look at my dresses?

FANNY. Of course, child. Run along.

BABETTE. (*Picks up the boxes.* DAVID *helps her.* SARA *crosses to* L. *of chair* U. C. *She goes to* R. *end of sofa* R.) I love dresses. I have a great fondness for materials and colors. Thank you, Grandma. (*She runs out of the room.*)

(JOSEPH *appears in the door* L.)

JOSEPH. There's a long distance operator with a long distance call for Mr. Muller. She wants to talk with him on the long distance phone.

KURT. (*As he goes* L.) Excuse me, please. (KURT *crosses* L. *quickly.* SARA *turns sharply to look at him.* TECK *looks up.* KURT *goes quickly out.* TECK *watches him go.* SARA *stands staring after him.*)

MARTHE. (*Laughs. As* KURT *passes sofa* L.) I feel the same way as Babbie. Come on, Sara. Let's try them on.

(SARA *does not turn.*)

TECK. You also have a new dress?

MARTHE. (*Looks at him.*) Yes. Fanny was kind to me, too.

TECK. (*Takes two steps away from fireplace.*) You are a very generous woman, Madame Fanny. Did you also give her a sapphire bracelet from Barstow's?

(MARTHE *crosses* D. *to chair* D. R.)

FANNY. I beg your ——

DAVID. (*Slowly.*) No. I gave Marthe the bracelet. And I understand that it is not any business of yours.

(FANNY *rises.* SARA *turns.*)

FANNY. Really, David ——

DAVID. Be still, Mama.

TECK. (*Rises, crosses to* L. C. *After a second.*) Did you tell him that, Marthe?

MARTHE. Yes.

TECK. (*Looks up at her.*) I shall not forgive you for that. (*Looks at* DAVID.) It is a statement which no man likes to hear from another man. You understand that? (*Playfully.*) That is the sort of thing about which we used to play at duels in Europe.

**47**

(SARA *crosses* U. *to behind piano keyboard.*)

DAVID. (*Comes toward him.*) We are not so musical comedy here. (*Crosses* U. *to behind sofa table* R.) And you are not in Europe.

TECK. (*Crosses* U. C.) Even if I were, I would not suggest any such action. I would have reasons for not wishing it.

DAVID. (*Crosses to behind chair* C.) It would be well for you not to suggest any action. And the reason for that is, you might get hurt.

TECK. (*Slowly.*) That would not be my reason. (*Turns to* MARTHE —*crosses* D. R. *to her—stops and speaks.*) Your affair has gone far enough ——

MARTHE. (*Sharply.*) It is not an affair ——

(FANNY *crosses* L. *to front of* L. *end of sofa* L.)

TECK. I do not care what it is. The time has come to leave here. Go upstairs and pack your things. (*She stands where she is* DAVID *crosses to below table* L. C.) Go on, Marthe.

MARTHE. (*Crosses* L. *to sofa table* R.; *to* DAVID. TECK *does not turn.*) I am not going with him. I told you that.

DAVID. I don't want you to go with him.

FANNY. (*Carefully.*) Really, David, aren't you interfering in this a good deal ——

DAVID. (*Looks to* FANNY. *Carefully.*) Yes, Mama. I am.

TECK. (*Turns to* MARTHE.) When you are speaking to me, please say what you have to say to me.

MARTHE. (*Comes to him, stands in front of the table.*) You are trying to frighten me. But you are not going to frighten me any more. (*Crosses* D. R. *to* TECK.) I will say it to you: I am not going with you. I am never going with you again.

TECK. (*Softly.*) If you do not fully mean what you say, or if you might change your mind, you are talking unwisely, Marthe.

MARTHE. I know that.

TECK. Shall we talk about it alone?

MARTHE. You can't make me go, can you, Teck?

TECK. No, I can't make you.

MARTHE. Then there's no sense talking about it.

TECK. Are you in love with him?

MARTHE. Yes.

FANNY. (*Sharply, taking steps* R.) Marthe! What is all this?

MARTHE. (*Sharply.*) I'll tell *you* about it in a minute.

DAVID. (*Crosses to* D. C. *chair.*) You don't have to explain anything to anybody.

TECK. (*Ignores him.*) Is he in love with you?

MARTHE. I don't think so. You won't believe it, because you can't believe anything that hasn't got tricks to it, but David hasn't much to do with this. I told you I would (DAVID *turns up and crosses to above chair* U. C., *turns back and watches scene* R.) leave some day, and I remember where I said it—(*Slowly.*) and why I said it.

TECK. I also remember. But I did not believe you, Marthe. I have not had much to offer you these last few years, but if we now had a little money and could go back . . .

MARTHE. No. I don't like you, Teck. I never have.

TECK. And I have always known it.

FANNY. (*Stiffly.*) I think your lack of affection should be discussed with more privacy.

(DAVID *turns sharply to* FANNY.)

DAVID. Mama!

(FANNY *crosses to sofa* L. *and sits.*)

MARTHE. (*Turning to* FANNY.) There's nothing to discuss. (*Turns to* TECK. FANNY *moves to* L. *end of sofa* L.) Strange. I've talked to myself about this scene for almost fifteen years. I knew a lot of things to say to you, and I used to lie awake at night, or walk along the street and say them. Now I don't want to. I guess you only want to talk that way when you're not sure what you can do. When you're sure, then what's the sense of saying it? " This is why and this is why and this ——" (*Very happily.*) But when you know you can do it, you don't have to say anything: you can just go. And I am going. There's nothing you can do. I would like you to believe that now.

TECK. Very well, Marthe. I think I made a mistake. I should not have brought you here. I believe you now. (*He moves up to decanter table.*)

MARTHE. (*After a pause, she looks to* DAVID. *Crosses to* C.) I'll move into—Washington, and ——

DAVID. (*Comes down to meet her* C. SARA *follows close behind* DAVID *on his* L.) Yes. Later, but I'd like you to stay here for a while with us, if you don't mind.

SARA. It would be better for you, Marthe ——

FANNY. It's very interesting that I am not being consulted about this. (*To* MARTHE, *as she goes to stand in front of sofa* L.) I have

49

nothing against you, Marthe. I am sorry for you, but I don't think —— (FANNY *sits* L. *end of sofa* L.)

MARTHE. Thank you, Sara, David. But I'd rather move in now. (*Comes toward* FANNY.) But, perhaps, I have something against you. Do you remember my wedding?

FANNY. Yes.

MARTHE. (*Sits* R. *of* FANNY.) Do you remember how pleased Mama was with herself? Brilliant Mama, handsome Mama— (FANNY *rises, steps* L.)—everybody thought so, didn't they? A seventeen year old daughter marrying a pretty good title, about to secure herself in a world that Mama liked.—She didn't ask me what I liked. And the one time I tried to tell her, she frightened me. (*Looks up.*) Maybe I've always been frightened. All my life.

TECK. Of course.

MARTHE. (*To* FANNY, *as if she had not heard* TECK.) I remember Mama's face at the wedding—it was *her* wedding, really, not mine.

FANNY. (*Sharply.*) You are very hard on your mother.

MARTHE. 1925. No, I'm not hard on her. I only tell the truth. She wanted a life for me, I suppose. It just wasn't the life I wanted for myself. (*Rises—sharply facing* FANNY.) And that's what you tried to do. With your children. In another way. Only SARA got away. And that made you angry—until so many years went by that you forgot.

FANNY. I don't usually mind people saying anything they think, but I find that ——

MARTHE. I don't care what you mind or don't mind. I'm in love with your son ——

(TECK *turns head away* R.)

FANNY. (*Very sharply.*) That's unfortunate ——

MARTHE. And I'm sick of watching you try to make him into his father. I don't think you even know you do it any more, and I don't think he knows it any more, either. And that's what's most dangerous about it.

(TECK *turns back to scene.*)

FANNY. (*Steps* D. L. *Very angrily.*) I don't know what you are talking about.

DAVID. I think you do. (*Smiles.*) You shouldn't mind hearing the

50

truth—and neither should I. (*Turns* R. *and crosses up to* U. C. *chair.*)

FANNY. (*Worried, sharply. Crosses below* MARTHE *to* DAVID.) David! What does all this nonsense mean? I ——

(TECK *crosses* D. R. *to above chair* D. R.)

MARTHE. (*To* FANNY.) Look. That pretty world Mama got me into was a tough world, see? I'm used to trouble. So don't try to interfere with me, because I won't let you. (*She goes to* DAVID.) Let's just have a good time. (*He leans down, takes both her hands, kisses them. Then slowly she turns away, starts to exit, crosses to* TECK.) You will also be going today?

TECK. Yes.

MARTHE. Then let us make sure we go in different directions, and do not meet again. Good-bye, Teck.

TECK. Good-bye, Marthe. You will not believe me, but I tried my best, and I am now most sorry to lose you.

MARTHE. Yes. I believe you. (*She moves out.*)

(*Silence for a moment.*)

FANNY. (*Crosses to* C. *and sits in chair* D. R. C.) Well, a great many things have been said in the last few minutes.

DAVID. (*Crosses to bell cord. To* TECK.) I will get Joseph to pack for you.

TECK. Do not bother. I will ring for him when I am ready. (KURT *comes in from the study door.* SARA *turns, stares at him, crosses to back of chair* U. C. *He does not look at her.*) It will not take me very long. (*Looking at* KURT.)

(KURT *crosses to below* R. *end of sofa* L.)

SARA. (*Crosses to* C.) What is it, Kurt?

KURT. It is nothing of importance, darling —— (*He looks quickly at* TECK.)

SARA. (*Crosses to* KURT.) Don't tell me it's nothing. I know the way you look when ——

KURT. (*Sharply.*) I said it was of no importance. I must get to California for a few weeks. That is all.

SARA. I ——

TECK. (*Turns, crosses up to get newspaper from secretary.*) It is in the afternoon paper, Herr Muller. (*Points to paper.*) I was waiting to find the proper moment to call it to your attention. (*He*

51

*moves toward table behind sofa* R., *as they all turn to watch him. He begnis to read.*) " Zurich, Switzerland: The Zurich papers today reprinted a despatch from the Berliner Tageblatt—on the capture of Colonel Max Freidank. Freidank is said (*Small sharp sound from* SARA. SARA *moves to* KURT.) to be the chief of the Anti-Nazi Underground Movement. Colonel Freidank has long been an almost legendary figure. The son of the famous General Freidank, he was a World War officer, and a distinguished physicist before the advent of Hitler." (*Throws paper on desk behind sofa* R.) That is all ——

SARA. (*Crying it out.*) Max ——

KURT. Be still, Sara.

TECK. (*Crosses above desk to* L. *end of it.*) They told me of it at the Embassy last night. They also told me that with him they had taken a man who called himself Ebber, and a man who called himself Triste. They could not find a man called Gotter. (*He starts again toward the door, moving* R. *slowly, above desk.*) I shall be a lonely man without Marthe. I am also a very poor one. I should like to have ten thousand dollars before I go.

DAVID. (*Taking step toward* TECK. *Carefully.*) You will make no loans in this house.

TECK. (*At* R. *of table* D. R. *Turns to* DAVID.) I was not speaking of a loan.

FANNY. (*Carefully.*) God made you not only a scoundrel but a fool. That is a dangerous combination.

DAVID. (*Suddenly starts toward* TECK.) Damn you . . . (*Crosses toward* TECK.)

KURT. Leave him alone. (*Tries to intercept* DAVID.) David! Leave him alone!

DAVID. (*Pushing past* KURT. *Angrily to* KURT.) Keep out of it. (*Starts toward* TECK *again.*) I'm beginning to see what Marthe meant. Blackmailing with your wife —— You ——

KURT. (*Very sharply.*) He is not speaking of his wife. (DAVID *turns to* KURT.) Or you. He means me. (*Looks at* TECK.) Is that correct?

(SARA *moves toward* KURT. DAVID *draws back, bewildered.* FANNY *comes toward them, staring at* TECK.)

TECK. Good. (*Crosses above* DAVID *to* R. *end of sofa* R.) It was necessary for me to hear you say it. You understand that? KURT. I understand it.

SARA. (*Crosses to* L. *of* KURT. *Frightened, softly.*) Kurt ——

DAVID. What is all this about? What the hell are you talking about?

TECK. (*Sharply for the first time.*) Be still. (DAVID *starts for* TECK, *restrains himself—crosses up to* L. *end of table* U. R. *To* KURT, *looks down at him.*) At your convenience. Your hands are shaking, Mr. Muller.

KURT. (*Quietly.*) My hands were broken: they are bad when I have fear.

(SARA *crosses slowly to front of* L. *end of sofa* L.)

TECK. I am sorry. I can understand that. It is not pleasant. (*Motions toward* FANNY *and* DAVID.) Perhaps you would like a little time to—I will go and pack, and be ready to leave. We will all find that more comfortable, I think. You should get yourself a smaller gun, Herr Muller. That pistol you have been carrying is big, and awkward. (*Crosses* R. *toward door* R.)

KURT. You saw the pistol when you examined my briefcase?

TECK. (*Smiles, turns back to* KURT.) You know that?

KURT. Oh, yes. Because I have the careful eye, through many years of needing it. And then you have not the careful eye. The pistol was lying to the left of a paper package, and when you leave, it is to the right of the package.

SARA. (*Steps toward* KURT.) Kurt! Do you mean that ——

KURT. (*Sharply.*) Please, darling, do not do that.

TECK. (*Puts his hand on* KURT'S *hip pocket, pats it.*) It is a German Army Luger?

KURT. Yes.

TECK. Keep it in your pocket, Herr Muller. You will have no need to use it. And, in any case, in any case, I am not afraid of it. You understand that?

KURT. (*Slowly, crosses to* TECK.) Yes, I understand that you are not a man of fears. That is strange to me, because I am a man who has so many fears.

TECK. (*Laughs, as he exits.*) Are you? That is most interesting. (*He exits* R.)

DAVID. (*Softly. Crosses* D. *to* L. *of* KURT.) What is this about, Kurt?

KURT. He knows who I am and what I do, and what I carry with me. (KURT *crosses* U. *and* L. *to behind table back of sofa* R.)

SARA. (*Carefully—steps* U. C.) What about Max?

KURT. (*Crosses to her, speaks when there.*) The telephone was

53

from Mexico. Ilse received a cable. Early on the morning of Monday they caught Ebber and Triste; an hour after, they took Max, in Berlin. (*She looks up at him, begins to shake her head. He presses her arm.*) Yes. It is hard. (KURT *turns away from her.*)
FANNY. (*Softly.*) You said he knew who you were and what you carried with you. I don't understand.

(SARA *crosses to behind piano keyboard.*)

KURT. (*Crosses to* L. *of* FANNY.) I am going to tell you: I am a German outlaw. I have been working with many others in an illegal organization. I have so worked for seven years. I am on what is called the Desired List. But I did not know I was worth ten thousand dollars. My price has risen.
DAVID. (*Slowly.*) And what do you carry with you?
KURT. Twenty-three thousand dollars. It has been gathered from the pennies and the nickels of the poor who do not like Fascism, and who believe in the work we do. (*Crosses slowly to below* L. *end of sofa* L.) I came here to bring Sara home, and to get the money. I had hopes to rest here for a while, and then ——
SARA. (*Slowly.*) And I had hopes someone else would take it back, and you would stay with us —— (*Shakes her head, then.*) Max is not dead?
KURT. No. The left side of his face is dead. (*Crosses* D. L. *Softly.*) It was a good face.
SARA. (*To* FANNY *and* DAVID, *as if she were going to cry.*) It was a very good face. He and Kurt —— (*A small move to* C.) In the old days . . . (*To* KURT.) After so many years. (*Steps toward* KURT.) If Max got caught, then nobody has a chance. Nobody. (*She suddenly turns and goes to sit* R. *end of sofa* L.)
DAVID. (*Steps* L. *toward* KURT.) He wants to sell what he knows to you? Is that right?
KURT. Yes.
FANNY. Wasn't it careless of you to leave twenty-three thousand dollars lying around to be seen?
KURT. No, it was not careless of me. It is in a locked briefcase. I have thus carried money for many years. There seemed no safer place than Sara's home. It was careless of you to have in your house a man who opens baggage and blackmails.
DAVID. (*Sharply.*) Yes. It was very careless.
FANNY. But you said you knew he'd seen it ——
KURT. The first day we arrived. What was I to do about it? He is

not a man who steals. This is a safer method. I knew it would come some other way. I have been waiting to see what the way would be. That is all I could do.

DAVID. (*To* FANNY.) What's the difference? It's been done. (*To* KURT.) If he wants to sell to you, he must have another buyer. Who?

KURT. The Embassy. Von Seitz, I think.

DAVID. You mean he has told Von Seitz about you and ——

KURT. No. I do not think he has told him anything. As yet. It would be foolish of him. He has probably only asked most guarded questions.

DAVID. But you're here. You're in this country. They can't do anything to you. They wouldn't be crazy enough to try it. Is your passport all right?

KURT. Not quite.

FANNY. Why not? Why isn't it?

KURT. (*Crosses to* U. C. *Wearily, as if he were bored.*) Because people like me are not given visas with such ease. And I was in a hurry to bring my wife and my children to safety. (*Turns—comes to* L. *of* FANNY. *Sharply.*) Madame Fanny, you must come to understand it is no longer the world you once knew.

DAVID. It doesn't matter. You're a political refugee. We don't turn back people like you. People who are in danger. You will give me your passport and tomorrow morning I'll (*Turns, crosses* R. *to* R. *of* R. *end of sofa* R.) see Barens. We'll tell him the truth —— (*Points to door.*) Tell de Brancovis to go to hell. There's not a damn thing he or anybody else can do.

SARA. (*Looks up at* KURT, *who is staring at her.*) You don't understand, David.

DAVID. There's a great deal I don't understand. But there's nothing to worry about.

SARA. (KURT *crosses to* SARA. *Still looking at* KURT.) Not much to worry about as long as Kurt is in this house. But he's not going to ——

KURT. The Count has made the guess that ——

SARA. That you will go back to get Ebber and Triste and Max out? Is that right, Kurt? Is that right?

KURT. Yes, darling, I must try. They were taken to Sonnenburg. Guards can be bribed. It has been done once before at Sonnenburg. We will try for it again. I must get back, Sara. I must start.

SARA. (*She gets up, comes to him. He holds her, puts his face in*

55

*her hair. She stands holding him, trying to speak without crying.*)
Of course you must go back. I guess I was trying to think it
wouldn't come. But —— (*To* FANNY *and* DAVID.) Kurt's got to go
back. He's got to go home. He's got to try to buy them out. He'll
do it, too. You'll see. (*She stops, breathes.*) It's hard enough to get
back. Very hard. (*Rises.*) But if they knew he was coming ——
They want Kurt bad. Almost as much as they wanted Max ——
And then there are hundreds of others, too —— (*Crosses
quickly to* KURT. *She puts her face down on his head.*) Don't be
scared, darling. You'll get back. You'll see. You've done it before
—you'll do it again. Don't be scared. You'll get Max out all
right. (*Gasps.*) And then you'll do his work, won't you? That's
good. That's fine. You'll do a good job, the way you've always
done. (*She holds his shoulder hard with her* L. *arm. She is crying
very hard. To* FANNY.) Kurt doesn't feel well. He was wounded
and he gets tired. (*To* KURT.) You don't feel well, do you?
(*Slowly, she is crying too hard now to be heard clearly.*) Don't
be scared, darling. You'll get home. Don't worry, you'll get home.
Yes, you will. (*She is holding his head close to her as the*)

## CURTAIN FALLS

# ACT III

SCENE: *The same. A half hour later.*

AT RISE: FANNY *is pacing from* L. *to* R. KURT *is at piano, his head resting on one hand. He is playing softly with the other.* SARA *is sitting very quietly on the* R. *end of couch* R. DAVID *is pacing on the terrace.* FANNY *crosses from* L. *to entry hall, back to* C., *then up to terrace door.*

FANNY. (*To* DAVID, *on the terrace.*) David, would you stop that pacing, please? (*To* KURT.) And would you stop that one-hand piano playing? Either play, or get up.

(KURT *gets up, crosses to* L. *of* SARA, *sits.* SARA *looks at him, gets up, crosses to the decanters, begins to make a drink.* FANNY *crosses to* R. *end of piano keyboard, leans on piano.*)

SARA. (*To* DAVID.) A drink?

DAVID. (*Comes in, closes door.*) What? Please. (*To* KURT. DAVID *crosses to back of chair* R. C., *leans on it.*) Do you intend to buy your friends out of jail?

KURT. I intend to try.

FANNY. (*Crosses* D. *to* D. L. C.) It's all very strange to me. I thought things were so well run that bribery and ——

KURT. (*Smiles.*) What a magnificent work Fascists have done in convincing the world that they are men from legends.

DAVID. They have done very well for themselves—unfortunately.

KURT. But not by themselves. Does it not make us all uncomfortable to remember that they came in on the shoulders of the most powerful men in the world? Of course. And so we would prefer to believe they are men from the planets. They are not. Let me reassure you. They are smart, they are sick, and they are cruel. But given men who know what they fight for —— (*Shrugs.*) You saw it in Spain. (FANNY *moves* L., *stops when he speaks. Laughs.*) I will console you: a year ago last month, at three o'clock in the morning, Freidank and I, with two elderly pistols, raided the home of the Gestapo chief in Konstanz, got what we

57

wanted and the following morning Freidank was eating his breakfast three blocks away, and I was over the Swiss border.

FANNY. (*Slowly.*) You are brave men.

KURT. I do not tell you the story to prove we are remarkable, but to prove they are not.

(SARA *is behind sofa* R. SARA *brings him a drink. Gives one to* DAVID. FANNY *crosses to sofa* L. *and sits* R. *end.* DAVID *crosses* L. *to* R. *of mail table* U. L. C.)

SARA. (*Softly, touching* KURT'S *shoulder.*) Kurt loves Max. I've always been a little jealous.

KURT. (*Puts his hand on hers.*) Always, since I came here, I have a dream: that he will walk in this room some day. How he would like it here, eh, Sara? (*To* FANNY.) He loves good food and wine, and you have books —— (*Laughs happily.*) He is fifty-nine years of age. And when he was fifty-seven he carried me on his back seven miles across the border. I had been hurt —— That takes a man, does it not?

FANNY. (*To* KURT.) You look like a sick man to me.

KURT. No. I am only tired. I do not like to wait. It will go.

SARA. (*Sharply.*) Oh, it's more than that. (*Crosses* R. *end of sofa* R.) This is one of the times you wonder why everything has to go against you. Even a holiday, the first in years ——

KURT. Waiting. It is waiting that is bad.

DAVID. Damn him, he's doing it deliberately.

KURT. It is then the corruption begins. Once in Spain I waited for two days until the planes would exhaust themselves. I think then why must our side fight always with naked hands? The spirit and the hands. All is against us but ourselves. Sometimes, it was as if you must put up your hands and tear the wings from the planes—and then it is bad.

SARA. (*To* D. R. *end of sofa* R.) You will not think that when the time comes. It will go.

KURT. Of a certainty.

FANNY. But does it have to go on being your hands?

KURT. For each man, his own hands. (*Looks at his hands.*) He has to sleep with them.

DAVID. (*Uncomfortably, as if he did not like to say it.*) That's right. I guess it's the way all of us should feel. But—(DAVID *steps* R. *to* C.) but you have a family. Isn't there somebody else who hasn't a wife and children ——?

KURT. Each could have his own excuse. Some love for the first time, some have bullet holes, some have fear of the camps, some are sick, many are getting older. (*Shrugs.*) Each could find a reason. And many find it. My children are not the only children in the world, even to me.

FANNY. That's noble of you, of course. But they are your children, nevertheless. And Sara, she ——

SARA. (*Softly.*) Mama ——

KURT. (*After a slight pause.* SARA *crosses* U. *and* L. *to behind* C. *of desk behind sofa* R.) One means always in English to insult with that word noble?

FANNY. Of course not, I ——

KURT. It is not noble. It is the way I must live. Good or bad, it is what I am. (*Turns deliberately to look at* FANNY.) And what I am is not what you wanted for your daughter, twenty years ago or now.

FANNY. You are misunderstanding me.

KURT. For our girl, too, we want a safe and happy life. And it is thus I try to make it for her. We each have our way. I do not convert you to mine.

DAVID. (*Crosses to back of chair* R. C.) You are very certain of your way.

KURT. (*Smiles.*) I seem so to you? Good.

(JOSEPH *appears in hall doorway. He is carrying valises, overcoats, and two small bags.*)

JOSEPH. (*To above table* D. R.) What'll I do with these, Miss Fanny?

(SARA *crosses to decanter table.*)

FANNY. They're too large for eating, aren't they? What were you thinking of doing with them?

JOSEPH. I mean, it's Fred's day off.

DAVID. All right. You drive him into town. (*Crosses to* L. *end of desk behind sofa* R., *puts down glass.*)

JOSEPH. Then who's going to serve at dinner?

FANNY. (*Impatiently.*) Belle will do it alone tonight.

JOSEPH. (*Crosses toward* FANNY, *stops* R. *of sofa* L.) No, she can't. Belle's upstairs packing with Miss Marthe. My, there's quite a lot of departing, ain't there?

(DAVID *crosses up to* U. L. C.)

59

FANNY. (*Very impatiently.*) All right, then cook can bring in dinner.

JOSEPH. I wouldn't ask her to do that, if I were you. She's mighty mad: the sink pipe is leaking. You just better wait for dinner 'til I get back from Washington.

(*Crosses* FANNY *to* L. *end of sofa.*)

FANNY. (*Shouting.*) We are not cripples and we were eating dinner in this house before you arrived to show us how to use the knife and fork. (JOSEPH *smiles.*) Go on. Put his things in the car. I'll ring for you when he's ready.

JOSEPH. You told me the next time you screamed to remind you to ask my pardon.

FANNY. You call that screaming?

JOSEPH. Yes'm.

FANNY. All right. I ask your pardon. Oh, go on, Go on.

JOSEPH. Yes'm. (*Exit* L., *closing door.*)

(TECK *appears in door. He is carrying his hat and the briefcase we have seen in Act 1.* SARA, *seeing briefcase, looks startled, looks quickly at* KURT. KURT *watches* TECK *as he comes toward him.* TECK *throws his hat on a chair, comes to table at which* KURT *is sitting, puts briefcase on table.* KURT *puts out his hand, puts it on briefcase, leaves it there.*)

TECK. (*Crosses to* R. *of* KURT, *to put briefcase on table* L. *of* KURT. KURT *reaches for case and holds it on table. Smiles at gesture.*) Nothing has been touched, Mr. Muller. I brought it from your room, for your convenience.

FANNY. (*Angrily.*) Why didn't you steal it? Since you don't seem to ——

TECK. (*Crosses to* C.) That would have been very foolish of me, Madame Fanny.

KURT. Very.

TECK. (*Turns to* KURT.) I hope I have not kept you waiting too long. I wanted to give you an opportunity to make any explanations ——

DAVID. (*Crosses to* L. *of* TECK. *Angrily.*) Does your price include listening to this tony conversation?

TECK. (*Turns to look at him.*) My price will rise if I have to spend the next few minutes being interrupted by your temper. I will do my business with Mr. Muller. And you will understand I will take from you no interruptions, no exclamations, no lectures, no opinions of what I am or what I am doing.

KURT. (*Quietly.*) You will not be interrupted.

TECK. (*Sits down at table with* KURT.) I have been curious about you, Mr. Muller. Even before you came here. Because Fanny and David either knew very little about you, which was strange, or would not talk very much about you, which was just as strange. Have you ever had come to you one of those insistent half-memories of some person or some place?

(SARA *slowly moves to sit* R. *end of sofa* R.)

KURT. (*Quietly, without looking up.*) You had such a half-memory of me?

TECK. (DAVID *crosses to chair* U. L. C., *turns and listens to* TECK.) Not even a memory, but something. The curiosity of one European for another, perhaps.

KURT. A most sharp curiosity. You lost no time examining—(*Pats case.*) this. You are an expert with locks?

TECK. No, indeed. Only when I wish to be.

FANNY. (*Rises. Angrily to* TECK.) I would like you out of this house as quickly as ——

TECK. (*Turns to her.*) Madame Fanny, I just asked Mr. David not to do that. I must now ask you. (*Leans forward to* KURT.) Herr Muller, I got the Desired List from Von Seitz without, of course, revealing anything to him. As you probably know it is quite easy for anybody to get. I simply told him that we refugees move in small circles and I might come across somebody on it. If, however, I have to listen to any more of this from any of you, I shall go immediately to him.

KURT. (*To* DAVID *and* FANNY.) Please allow the Count to do this in his own way. It will be best.

(FANNY *sits again.*)

TECK. (*Takes sheet of paper from pocket.*) There are sixty-three names on this list. I read them carefully, I narrow the possibilities and under " G " I find Gotter. (*Begins to read.*) " Age: forty to forty-five. About six feet. One hundred seventy pounds. Birthplace unknown to us. Original occupation unknown to us, although he seems to know Munich and Dresden. Schooling unknown to us. Family unknown to us. No known political connections. No known trade union connections. Many descriptions; few of them in agreement, and none of them of great reliability. Equally unreliable, though often asked for, were Paris, Copenhagen, Brussels police descriptions. Only points on which there is agreement: married to a foreign woman, (SARA'S *hand grasps* KURT'S.) either American or English; three children; has used name of Gotter, Thomas Bodmer, Karl Francis. Thought to have left Germany in 1933, and to have joined Max Freidank shortly after. Worked closely with Freidank, perhaps directly under his orders. Known to have crossed border in 1934—February, May, June, October." (SARA *begins to rise from table.* KURT *puts his hand over hers. She sits down again.*) "Known to have again crossed border with Max Freidank in 1935—August, twice in October, November, January ——"

KURT. (*Smiles.*) The report is unreliable. It would have been impossible for God to have crossed the border that often.

TECK. (*Looks up. Then looks back at list.*) Yes? "In 1934, outlaw radio station, announcing itself as Radio European, begins to be heard. Station was located in Dusseldorf; the house of a restaurant waiter was searched, and nothing was found. Radio heard during most of 1934 and 1935. In an attempt to locate it, two probable Communists killed in the tool-house of a farm near Bonn. In three of the broadcasts, Gotter known to have crossed border immediately before and after. Radio again became active in early part of 1936. Active attempt made to locate Freidank. Gotter believed to have then appeared in Spain with Madrid Government army, in one of the German brigades, and to be a brigade commander under previously used name of Bodmer. Known to have stayed in France the first months of 1938. Again crossed German border some time during week when Hitler's Hamburg radio speech interrupted and went off the air." (*Looks up.*) That was a daring deed, Herr Muller. It caused a great scandal. I remember. It amused me.

KURT. It was not done for that reason.

TECK. No? "Early in 1939, informer in Konstanz reported Gotter's entry, carrying money which had been exchanged in Paris and Brussels. Following day, Konstanz Gestapo raided for spy list by two men —— (KURT *turns to look at* FANNY *and* DAVID, *smiles.*) My God, Mr. Muller, that job took two good men.

SARA. (*Angrily.*) Even you admire them.

TECK. Even I. Now, I conclude, a week ago, that you are Gotter, Karl Francis ——

KURT. Please. Do not describe me to myself again.

TECK. And that you will be traveling home (*Points to brief-case.*)—with this. But you seem in no hurry, and so I must wait. Last night when I hear that Freidank has been taken, I guess that you will now be leaving. Not for California. I will tell you, free of charge, Herr Muller, that they have got no information from Freidank or the others.

KURT. Thank you. But I was sure they would not. I know all three most well. They will take—what will be given them.

TECK. (*Looks down. Softly.*) There is a deep sickness in the German character, Herr Muller. A pain-love, a death-love ——

DAVID. (*Very angrily.*) Oh, for God's safe, spare us your moral judgments.

FANNY. (*Very sharply.*) Yes. They are sickening. Get on!

KURT. Fanny and David are Americans and they do not understand our world—as yet. (*Turns to* DAVID *and* FANNY.) All Fascists are not of one mind, one stripe. There are those who give the orders, those who carry out the orders, those who watch the orders being carried out. Then there are those who are half in, half hoping to come in. They are made to do the dishes and clean the boots. Frequently, they come in high places and wish now only to survive. They came late; some because they did not jump in time, some because they were stupid, some because they were shocked at the crudity of the German evil, and preferred their own evils, and some because they were fastidious men. For those last, we may well some day have pity. They are lost men, their spoils are small, their day is gone. (*To* TECK.) Yes?

TECK. (*Slowly.*) Yes. (DAVID *moves to front of chair* U. L. C.) You have the understanding heart. It will get in your way some day.

KURT. (*Smiles.*) I will watch it.

(DAVID *sits in chair* U. L. C.)

TECK. We are both men in trouble, Herr Muller. The world, un-gratefully, seems to like your kind even less than it does mine. (*Leans forward.*) Now. Let us do business. You will not get back if Von Seitz knows you are going.

KURT. You are wrong. Instead of crawling a hundred feet an hour in deep night, I will walk across the border with as little trouble as if I were a boy again on a summer walking trip. There are many men they would like to have. I would be allowed to walk directly to them, if I were so big a fool, or if I found it necessary—until they had all the names, and all the addresses —— (FANNY *rises.*) *Roumanians* would pick me up ahead of time. *Germans* would not.

TECK. (*Smiles.*) Still the national pride?

KURT. Why not? For that which is good.

FANNY. (*Comes over, very angrily, to* TECK.) I have not often in my life felt what I feel now. Whatever you are, and however you became it, the picture of a man selling the lives of other men ——

TECK. Is very ugly, Madame Fanny. I do not do it without some shame, and I must therefore sink my shame in large money. (FANNY *slaps him with her handkerchief.* TECK *rises.* DAVID *rises.* FANNY *crosses to mail table and drops handkerchief on it.* TECK *turns to* KURT. *Violently, pointing to briefcase.*) The money is here. (TECK *sits.*) For ten thousand dollars you go back to save your friends; nobody will know that you are gone. (*Slowly, deliberately,* KURT *begins to shake his head.* TECK *waits, then carefully.*) What?

KURT. This money is going home with me. It was not given to me to save my life, and I shall not so use it. It is to save the lives and further the work of more than I. It is important to me to carry on that work: it is important to me to save the lives of three valuable men, and to do that with all possible speed. And, (*Sharply.*) Count de Brancovis, the first morning we arrived in this house my children wanted their breakfast with great haste. That is because the evening before we had been able only to buy milk and buns for them. If I would not touch this money for them, I would not touch it for you. (*Very sharply.*) It goes back with me. The way it is. And if it does not get back, it is because I will not get back.

(*There is a long pause.*)

TECK. Then I do not think you will get back, Herr Muller. You are a brave one, but you will not get back.

KURT. (*As if he were very tired.*) I will send to you a postal card, and tell you about my bravery.

DAVID. (*Coming toward* KURT.) Is it true that if this swine talks you and the others will be ——

SARA. (*Very softly.*) Caught and killed. Of course. If they're lucky enough to get killed quickly. (*Quietly, points to the table.*) You should have seen those hands in 1935. (*Turns* R. *and rises. Crosses to* R. *end of sofa* R., *facing upstage.*)

FANNY. (*Violently, to* DAVID.) We'll give him the money. For God's sake, let's give it to him and get him out of here.

DAVID. (*Crosses to* SARA.) Do you want him to go back?

SARA. Yes. (KURT *looks up to her.*) I do.

DAVID. All right. (*Goes to her, arm around her.*) You're a good girl, Sara.

KURT. That is true. Brave and good, my Sara. She is everything. Handsome and gay and —— (*Puts his hand over his eyes.*)

(SARA *turns away.*)

DAVID. (*Around desk to* L. *of* TECK. *After a second, comes to stand near* TECK.) If we give you the money, what is to keep you from selling to Von Seitz?

TECK. I do not like your thinking I would do that. But ——

DAVID. (*Tensely.*) Look here. I'm sick of what you'd like or wouldn't like. And I'm sick of your talk. We'll get this over with now, without any more fancy talk from you, or as far as I am concerned you can get out of here without my money and sell to any buyer you can find. I can't take much more of you, at any cost.

TECK. (*Smiles.*) It is your anger which delays us. I was about to say that I understood your fear that I would go to Von Seitz, and I would suggest that you give me a small amount of cash now, and a check dated a month from now. In a month, Herr Muller should be nearing home, and he can let you know. If you should not honor the check because Herr Muller is already in Germany, Von Seitz will pay a little something for a reliable description. I will take my chance on that. You will now say that I can do that in any case—and that is the chance you will take.

DAVID. (*Crosses up to behind table* R. C. *Looks at* KURT, *who does not look up.*) Is a month enough? For you to get back?

KURT. I do not know!

DAVID. (*To* TECK.) Two months from today. How do you want the cash and how do you want the check?

TECK. *One month from today.* That I will not discuss. One month. Please decide now.

DAVID. (*Sharply.*) All right. (*To* TECK.) How do you want it?

TECK. Seevnty-five hundred dollars in a check. Twenty-five hundred in cash.

DAVID. I haven't anywhere near that much cash in the house.

(*Turns, crosses* L.) Leave your address, and I'll send it to you in the morning.

TECK. (DAVID *turns back. Laughs.*) Address? I have no address, and I wish it now. Madame Fanny has some cash in her sitting-room safe.

FANNY. Have you investigated that, too?

TECK. (*Laughs.*) No. You once told me you always kept money in the house.

DAVID. (*To* FANNY.) How much have you got upstairs?

FANNY. I don't know. About fifteen or sixteen hundred.

TECK. Very well. That will do. Make the rest in the check.

DAVID. Get it, Mama, please. (*He starts toward library door.*)

FANNY. (*Looks carefully at* TECK.) Years ago somebody said that being Roumanian was not a nationality, but a profession. The years have brought no change. (*Starts for the hall exit* R. DAVID *closes door* L. FANNY *stops as* KURT *speaks.*)

KURT. (*Softly.*) Being a Roumanian *aristocrat* is a profession.

(FANNY *exits. After her exit, there is silence.* KURT *does not look up,* SARA *does not move.*)

TECK. (*Awkwardly.*) The new world has left the room. (*Looks up at them.*) I feel less discomfort with you. We are Europeans, born to trouble, and understanding it.

KURT. My wife is not a European.

TECK. Almost. (*Points upstairs.*) They are young. The world has gone well for most of them. For us—(*Smiles.*) the three of us—we are like peasants watching the big frost. Work, trouble, ruin —— (*Shrugs.*) But no need to call curses at the frost. There it is, there it will be again, always—for us.

SARA. (*Gets up, moves to the window, looks out.*) You mean my husband and I do not have angry words for you. What for? We know how many there are of you. They don't yet. My mother and brother feel shocked that you are in their house. For us—we have seen you in so many houses. (*Crosses* U. L. *to terrace window* L.)

TECK. I do not say you *want* to understand me, Mrs. Muller. I say only that you do.

SARA. Yes. You are not difficult to understand.

KURT. (*Slowly gets up, stands stiffly, as if to adjust his back. Then he moves toward decanter table.*) Whiskey?

TECK. No, thank you. (*He turns his head to watch* KURT *move.* *He turns back.*)

KURT. (*Picks up sherry decanter.*) Sherry?

TECK. (*Nods.*) Thank you, I will.

KURT. (*As he pours. Removes decanter top.*) You, too, wish to go back to Europe? (*Pours sherry.*)

TECK. Yes.

KURT. But they do not much want you. Not since the Budapest oil deal of '31. (*Puts down decanter and glass.*)

TECK. You seem as well informed about me as I am about you.

(KURT *moves to upstage side of decanter table.*)

KURT. That must have been a conference of high comedy, that one. Everybody trying to guess whether Kessler was working for Fritz Thyssen, and what Thyssen *really* wanted—and whether this "National Socialism" was a smart blind of Thyssen's, and where was Wolff—(*Picks up whiskey decanter and glass.*) I should like to have seen you and your friends. It is too bad: you guessed an inch off, eh?

TECK. More than an inch.

(KURT *pours whiskey.*)

KURT. And Kessler has a memory? (*Puts down decanter, picks up syphon and adds soda. Almost playfully.*) I do not think Von Seitz would pay you money for a description of a man who has a month to travel. But I think he would pay you in a visa, and a cable to Kessler. I think you want a visa almost as much as you want money. Therefore, I conclude you will try for the money here, and the visa from Von Seitz. (*He stirs whiskey and soda.*) I cannot get anywhere near Germany in a month and you know it. (*He picks up sherry glass and comes toward table.*) I have been bored with this talk of paying you money. If they are willing to try you on this fantasy, I am not. Whatever made you think I would take such a chance? (*Puts down whiskey glass.*) Or *any* chance? You're a gambler. (*Offers* TECK *sherry glass.*) But you should not gamble with your life. (*Throws sherry glass to floor.*) TECK *has turned to stare at him, made a half-motion as if to rise. As he does so, and on the words, " gamble with your life," KURT upsets the glass. With his free left arm, he presses down on* TECK's *left arm, begins to move his right hand to hit* TECK's *jaw. As he does so,* TECK *makes a violent effort to rise.* KURT *throws himself*

**67**

on TECK, *pressing him to the chair.* KURT *continues to punch* TECK *on the side jaw and head, and pushes him away. The chair turns over, and goes to the floor.* KURT *leans down, begins to lift* TECK *from the floor. As he does so* JOSHUA *appears in the hall entrance. He is washed and ready for dinner. As he reaches the door, he stops, sees the scene, stands quietly as if he were waiting for orders.* KURT *begins to balance* TECK, *to balance himself.* KURT, *to* JOSHUA, *in German.*) Mach die Tür auf! (JOSHUA *runs toward doors, opens them, stands waiting.*) Bleibt da. Macht die Ture zu. (KURT *begins to move out through terrace. When he is outside the doors,* JOSHUA *closes them quickly, stands looking at his mother.*)

SARA. (*Leans on chair* U. L. C.) There's trouble.

JOSHUA. Do not worry. I will go up now. I will pack. In ten minutes all will be ready. I will say nothing. I will get the children ready —— (*He starts quickly for hall, turns for a second to look toward terrace doors. Then, almost with a sob.*) This was a nice house —— (*Starts* R. *suddenly.*)

SARA. (*Softly.* JOSHUA *stops at* SARA'S *voice.*) We're not going this time, darling. There's no need to pack.

JOSHUA. (*To* R. *end of sofa* R. *Stares at her, puzzled.*) but Papa ——

SARA. Go upstairs, Joshua. Take Babbie and Bodo in your room, and close the door. Stay there until I call you. (*He looks at her, then slowly starts toward the steps.* SARA *slowly sits in chair* U. L. C.) There's nothing to be frightened of, darling. Papa is all right. (*Then very softly, childishly.*) Papa is going home.

JOSHUA. Home? To Germany?

SARA. Yes.

JOSHUA. Oh. Alone?

SARA. Alone. (*Very softly.*) Don't say anything to the children. He will tell them himself.

JOSHUA. I won't.

SARA. (*As he hesitates.*) I'm all right. Go upstairs now. (*He moves slowly out* R., *she watches him, he disappears. For a moment she sits quietly. Then she gets up, moves to terrace doors, stands with her hands pressed against them. Then she crosses, picks up chair, places it behind table, picks up glass, puts it on table. As if without knowing what she is doing, she wipes table with her handkerchief.*)

(*After a second,* DAVID *comes in from* L. *followed by* FANNY, *who comes in from hall* R. DAVID *stops, puzzled.*)

68

DAVID. (*To* L. *end of sofa* L.) Where —— Is he upstairs?

SARA. They went outside.

FANNY. (DAVID *to* R. *end of sofa* L.) Outside? They went outside? What are they doing, picking a bouquet together? (FANNY *goes to* R. *of table* D. R.)

SARA. (*Without turning.*) They just went outside.

(DAVID *stands looking at her.*)

DAVID. What's the matter, Sara?

(SARA *goes to secretary and looks for a number in phone book.*)

FANNY. (*Counts some bills.*) Eleven hundred, eleven hundred and fifty, twelve, twelve-fifty ——

DAVID. (*Crosses toward* FANNY.) For God's sake stop counting that money.

FANNY. All right. (*She sits* R. *of table.*) I'm nervous. And I don't like to think of giving him too much.

SARA. (*Dialing.*) That's very kind of you and Mama. All that money —— Hello. What time is your next plane? Oh, to—South. To El Paso, or Brownsville—yes.

DAVID. (*To* FANNY. *Puts check on table* D. R.) Is Joseph ready?

FANNY. I don't know. I'd told him I'd call him.

(DAVID *begins to cross to bell cord.*)

SARA. To Brownsville? Yes. Yes. That's all right. At what time? Yes. No. The ticket will be picked up at the airport. (*She looks up.*) No. David. Don't call Joseph. *David! Please!* (*He draws back, stares at her. Looking at him, she goes on with the conversation.*) Ritter. R-i-t-t-e-r. From Chicago. Yes. Yes. (*She hangs up.*)

DAVID. (*Crosses to* C.) Sara! What's happening? What is all this? (*She does not answer.*) Where is Kurt? What —— (*He starts for terrace door.*)

SARA. David. (*Stopping him* U. C. FANNY *rises.*) *Don't go out.*

FANNY. (SARA *crosses to chair* U. L. C. *and leans against it.*) Sara! What's happening ——

SARA. For seven years now, day in, day out, men have crossed the German border. They are always in danger. And they always may be going in to die. Did you ever see the face of a man who never knows if this day will be the last day? (*Softly.*) Don't go out on the terrace, David. Leave Kurt alone.

FANNY. (*Softly.*) Sara! What is it?

69

SARA. (*Quietly.*) For them, it may be torture and it may be death. Some day, when it's all over, maybe there'll be a few of them left to celebrate. There aren't many of Kurt's age left. He couldn't take a chance on them. They wouldn't have liked it. (*Suddenly, violently.*) He'd have had a bad time trying to explain to them that because of this house, and this nice town, and my mother and my brother, he took chances with their work and with their lives. (*Quietly.*) Sit down, Mama. I think it's all over now. (*To* DAVID.) There's nothing you can do about it. It's the way it had to be.

DAVID. (*Quietly.*) GOD!

FANNY. (*Sits slowly.*) Do you mean what I think you——?

SARA. (*She turns, looks out toward doors. After a pause.*) He's going away tonight, and he's never coming back any more. (*In a sing-song.*) Never, never, never. (*She looks down at her hands, as if she were very interested in them.*) I don't like to be alone at night. I guess everybody in the world's got a time in the day they don't like. Me, it's right before I go to sleep. And now it's going to be for always. All the rest of my life. (*She looks up as* KURT *comes in from terrace.* KURT *stands looking at her.*) I've told them. There is an eight-thirty plane going as far south as Brownsville. I've made you a reservation in the name of Ritter.

KURT. (*He comes down to her. He puts his hand on her shoulder, she bends her head to touch it.*) Liebe Sara! (*Then he goes to table at which* FANNY *is sitting. To* FANNY.) It is hard for you, eh? (*He pats her hand.*) I am sorry.

FANNY. (*Without knowing why, she takes her hand away.*) Hard? I don't know. I—I don't—I don't know what I want to say.

KURT. Before I come in, I stand and think. I say, I will make Fanny and David understand. I say, How can I? Does one understand a killing? No. To hell with it, I say. I do what must be done. I have long sickened of words, when I see the men who live by them. What do you wish to make them understand? I ask myself. Stand here. Just stand here. What are you thinking? Say it to them as it comes to you. And this is how it came to me: when you kill in a war it is not so lonely; and I remember a cousin I have not seen for many years; and a melody comes back and I begin to make it with my fingers; a staircase in a house in Bonn years ago; Sara in a hundred places. Shame on us. Thousands of years and we cannot yet make a world. I have stopped a man's life. (*Points to place on couch where he was sitting opposite* TECK.) I sit here. I listen to him. You will not believe—but I

70

pray I will not have to touch him. Then I know I will have to. I know that if I do not, it's only that I pamper myself, and risk the lives of others. I want you from the room. I know what I must do. (*Loudly.*) All right. Shall I now pretend sorrow? Shall I now pretend that it is not I who act thus? No! I do it. I have done it. And I will do it again. And I will keep my hope that we may make a world where all men can die in bed. I have great hate for the violent: they are the sick of the world. (*He sinks to sofa, softly.*) Maybe I am sick now, too.

SARA. You aren't sick. Stop that. It's late. You must go soon.

KURT. (*Looks up at her.*) Maybe all that I have ever wanted is a land that would let me have you. (*Then without looking away from her, he puts out his hands and takes hers. She sits beside him quickly. Rises.*) I will say good-bye now to my children. (*Turns up to DAVID.*) Then I am going to take your car. (*Motions with his head.*) I will take him with me. After that, it is up to you. Two ways: you can let me go and keep silent. I believe I can hide him and the car. At the end of two days, if they have not been found, you will call the police. You will tell as much of the truth as is safe for you to say. Tell them the last time you saw us we were on our way to Washington. You did not worry at the absence, we might have rested there. Two crazy foreigners fight, one gets killed, you know nothing of the reason. I will have left the gun, there will be no doubt who did the killing. If you will give me those two days, I think I will be far enough away from here. If the car is found before then—(*Shrugs.*) I will still try to move with speed. (*Turns to FANNY.*) And all that will make you, for yourselves, part of a murder. For the world, I do not think you will be in bad trouble. (*He pauses. Crosses down to FANNY.*) Then there is another way. You can call your police now. You can tell them the truth. I will not get home. (*To SARA.*) I wish to see the children now. (*She goes out into hall. After a second, KURT goes to L. to chair L.*)

(*There is silence. After a second, FANNY begins to speak.*)

FANNY. What are you thinking, David?

DAVID. I don't know.

FANNY. I was thinking about my Joshua. I was thinking that a few months before he died we were sitting out there. (*Points to terrace.*) "Fanny," he said, "the Renaissance American is dying, the Renaissance man is dying." I said, "What do you mean?" although I knew what he meant, I always knew. " Renaissance man," he said, " is a man who wants to know. He wants to know how fast a bird will fly, how thick is the crust of the earth, what made Iago evil, how to plough a field. He knows there is no dignity to a mountain, if there is no dignity to man. (KURT *turns to look at her.*) You cannot put that in a man, but once it is *really* there, and he will fight for it, you can put your trust in him."

DAVID. (*Looks at* FANNY.) You're a smart woman sometimes. (*Rises, crosses to* KURT.) Don't worry about things here. My soul doesn't have to be so nice and clean. (SARA *and* JOSHUA *come down stairs.*) I'll take care of it. You'll have your two days. And good luck to you.

FANNY. You go with my blessing, too. I like you.

SARA. (*To* R. *end of sofa* R.) See? I come from good stock.

(KURT *has looked at* DAVID. *Then he begins to smile. Nods to* DAVID. *Turns, smiles at* FANNY.)

FANNY. Do you like me?

(*On her speech,* BODO *comes in from hall.*)

KURT. (*Crosses to* D. L. C.) Very much, Madame.

FANNY. Would you be able to cash that check?

KURT. (*Laughs.*) Oh, no.

FANNY. Then take the cash. I, too, would like to contribute—to your work.

KURT. (*Slowly.*) Thank you.

BODO. (*To* KURT.) You like Grandma? (*Moves to* FANNY.) I thought you would, with time. I like her, too. Sometimes she dilates with screaming, but —— Dilates is correct?

(JOSHUA *stands away from others, looking at* KURT. KURT *turns to look at him.*)

JOSHUA. Alles in Ordnung?

(BABETTE *comes in from the hall.*)

KURT. Alles in Ordnung.

BODO. (*Crosses to* KURT.) What? What does that mean—all is well?

(KURT *crosses up to front of chair* U. L. C. *There is an awkward silence.*)

BABETTE. (*To above and* L. *of* FANNY. *As if she sensed it.*) We are all clean for dinner. But nobody else is clean. And I have on Grandma's dress to me ——

FANNY. (*Rises, crosses behind* BABETTE *to* KURT *and gives him money.*) Of course. And you look very pretty. You're a pretty little girl, Babbie. (FANNY *goes to behind desk, behind sofa* R., *tears check, sits.*)

(KURT *sits in chair* U. L. C.)

BODO. (*Looks around the room.*) What is the matter? Everybody is acting like such a ninny. (*Crosses up to* KURT.) I got that word from Grandma.

KURT. Come here. . . . Come. (*They look at him. Then slowly* BABETTE *comes toward him, followed by* JOSHUA, *to stand at side of* KURT'S *chair.* KURT *takes* BODO *on his lap,* BABETTE *to his* L., JOSHUA *to his* R.) We have said many good-byes to each other, eh? We must now say another. (SARA *moves up to* R. *of desk. As they stare at him, he smiles, slowly, as if it were difficult.*) This time I leave you with good people to whom I believe you, also, will be good. (*Half-playfully.*) Would you allow me to give away my share in you until I come back?

BABETTE. (*Slowly.*) If you would like it.

KURT. Good! To Mama, her share. My share to Fanny and David. It is all and it is the most I have to give. (*Laughs.*) There. I have made a will, eh? Now. We will not joke. I have something to say to you. It is important for me to say it.

JOSHUA. (*Softly.*) You are talking to us as if we were children.

KURT. (*Turns to look at him.*) Am I, Joshua? I wish you were children. I wish I could say, Love your mother, do not eat too many sweets, clean your teeth . . . (*Draws* BODO *to him.*) I cannot say these things. You are not children. I took it all away from you.

BABETTE. We have had a most enjoyable life, Papa.

KURT. (*Smiles, pats her hand and holds it to his cheek.*) You are a gallant little liar. And I thank you for it. I have done something bad today ——

FANNY. (*Shocked, sharply.*) Kurt ——

SARA. Don't, Mama.

(BODO *and* BABETTE *have looked at* FANNY *and* SARA, *puzzled. Then they have turned again to look at* KURT.)

KURT. It is not to frighten you. In a few days, your mother and David will tell you.

BODO. You could not do a bad thing.

BABETTE. (*Proudly.*) You could not.

KURT. (*Shakes his head.*) Now let us get straight together. The four of us. Do you remember when we read Les Miserables? Do you remember that we talked about it afterwards, and Bodo got candy on Mama's bed?

BODO. I remember.

KURT. Well. He stole bread. The world is out of shape, we said, when there are hungry men. And until it gets in shape, men will always steal and lie and—(*A little more slowly.*) kill. But for whatever reason it is done, and whoever does it—you understand me—it is all bad. I want you to remember that. Whoever does it, it is bad. (*Then very gaily.*) But you will live to see the day when it will not have to be. All over the world, in every place and every town, there are men who are going to make sure it will not have to be. They want what I want: a childhood for every child. For my children, and I, for theirs. (*He picks BODO up, rises, moves toward hall, followed by BABETTE and JOSHUA.*) Think of that. It will make you happy. In every town and every village and every mud hut in the world, there is always a man who loves children, who will fight to make a good world for them. And now good-bye. Wait for me. I shall try to come back for you. (*He is above table D. R.*) Or you shall come to me. At Hamburg, the boat will come in. It will be a fine, safe land—I will be waiting on the dock. And there will be the three of you and Mama and Fanny and David. And I will have ordered an extra big dinner and we will show them what my Germany can be like —— (*He has put BODO down. He leans down, presses his face in BABETTE's hair. Tenderly, as her mother has done earlier, she touches his hair.*)

JOSHUA. (*Slowly.*) Of course. That is the way it will be. Of course. But—but if you should find yourself delayed . . . (*Very slowly.*) Then I will come to you. Mama.

SARA. (*She has turned away.*) I heard you, Joshua.

KURT. (*He kisses BABETTE.*) Gute Nacht, Liebling!

BABETTE. Gute Nacht, Papa. Mach's gut! (BABETTE *goes up steps.*)

KURT. (*Leans to kiss BODO.*) Good night, Baby.

BODO. Good night, Papa. Mach's gut! (BODO *follows* BABETTE *slowly.*)

74

KURT. (*Kisses* JOSHUA.) Good night, son.

JOSHUA. Good night, Papa. Mach's gut! (*He begins to climb the steps.*)

(KURT *stands watching them, smiling. When they disappear, he turns to* DAVID.)

KURT. (FANNY *rises, crosses to* U. R. C. *Crosses to* DAVID.) Good-bye, and thank you.

DAVID. Good-bye, and good luck.

KURT. (*He moves up to* FANNY, *he offers his hand.*) Good-bye. I have five children, eh?

FANNY. Yes, you have. (*He bends and kisses her hand.* FANNY *goes to behind desk.*)

(SARA *comes to* KURT.)

KURT. (*Slowly.*) Men who wish to live have the best chance to live. I wish to live. I wish to live with you.

SARA. For twenty years. It is as much for me today —— (*Takes his arms.*) Just once, and for all my life. (*She nods.*) Come back for me, darling. If you can.

KURT. (*Simply.*) I will try. (*He pulls her toward him. They kiss. She breaks away, reaches for his briefcase and gives it to him. He takes it and turns.*) Good-bye to you all. (*He exits.*)

(SARA *sits down, looks up at* DAVID, *smiles. He comes to her, kisses her, moves away again. After a second, there is the sound of a car starting. They sit listening to it. Gradually the noise begins to go off into the distance. A second later* JOSHUA *appears.*)

JOSHUA. Mama. (*She looks up. He is very tense.*) Bodo cries. Babette looks very queer. I think you should come.

SARA. (*Gets up, slowly.*) I'm coming. (*And goes up stairs.*)

JOSHUA. (*To* FANNY *and* DAVID. *Still very tense.*) Bodo talks so fancy, we forget sometimes he is a baby. (*He goes up stairs.*)

(FANNY *and* DAVID *watch them.*)

FANNY. (*After a minute.*) Well, here we are. We're shaken out of the magnolias, eh?

DAVID. (*Laughs.*) Yes, so we are.

FANNY. Tomorrow will be a hard day. But we'll have Babbie's birthday dinner. And we'll have music afterwards. You can be the audience. You'd better go up to Marthe now. Be as careful as you can. She'd better stay here for a while. I dare say I can stand it.

DAVID. (*Turns, smiles.*) Even your graciousness is ungracious, Mama.

FANNY. I do my best. Well, I think I shall go and talk to Anise. (*Rises, starts* R.) I like Anise best when I don't feel well. (*She begins to move off.*)

DAVID. Mama. (*She turns.*) We are going to be in for trouble. You understand that?

FANNY. I understand it very well. We will manage. You and I. I'm not put together with flour paste. And neither are you—I am happy to learn.

DAVID. (*He begins to laugh.*) Good night, Mama.

(*As she moves out . . .*)

## THE CURTAIN COMES DOWN

# Le Petit Géant

### Caroline Merola

# 1

# Le pique-nique des grands

Pierre, Jean et Jacques ont organisé un pique-nique. C'est pour samedi matin. Ils ont invité tous leurs amis, mais ils ne veulent pas de leur petite sœur Margot.

– Je veux aller avec vous!

Pierre répond:

– Pas question! Il n'y aura que des grands de cinquième et de sixième année.

Jean ajoute:

– De quoi on aurait l'air avec une petite puce de sept ans comme toi?

5

Jacques rigole:

– Et puis, comment viendrais-tu? Tu n'as même pas de bicyclette.

Les trois frères rient de bon cœur. Margot est vexée. Elle leur jette un regard noir:

– Je peux prendre la vieille bicyclette de Jean. Je sais pédaler.

Pierre répond:

– De toute façon tu ne pédales pas assez vite, on passerait notre temps à t'attendre. Tu n'as qu'à organiser un pique-nique avec tes amis.

Margot insiste:

– Non! Je veux aller avec vous! Je veux aller avec les grands. Je connais tous vos amis. Ils vont être d'accord.

Jean l'interrompt:

– Non, tu ne connais pas tout le monde. Tu n'as jamais rencontré Aldo le géant.

Puis il se met à ricaner.

Margot ouvre grand les yeux:

– Qui ça? Aldo le géant? Vous connaissez un géant?

Pierre, Jean et Jacques se regardent et font un drôle de sourire. Ils répondent:

– Bien sûr, un géant. Un immense géant comme tu n'en as jamais vu!

Puis ils éclatent de rire.

– Je ne vous crois pas, dit Margot.

Mais elle se demande bien qui est ce mystérieux Aldo.

# 2

# Le grand jour

Le samedi matin est enfin arrivé. Il fait très beau, pas trop chaud. Les frères de Margot ont préparé un succulent dîner: du poulet, des noix, des petits jus, des fruits. Leur mère leur a même fait de bons biscuits au chocolat.

Margot a le cœur gros quand elle voit les amis de ses frères arriver: Léa-la-frisée; P'tit-Louis; les jumelles Brisebois, Lili et Loulou; et Okédou. Il s'appelle Philippe, mais il dit toujours «Ok-dou». Alors c'est devenu son surnom.

Maintenant, tout le monde est là, sauf le prétendu géant.

Margot croit de plus en plus que ses frères lui ont fait une blague. Elle dit d'un ton moqueur:

– Êtes-vous sûrs de lui avoir donné la bonne adresse, à votre géant?

– De qui parles-tu? demande Jean. Ah oui, c'est vrai, Aldo… On l'avait oublié, celui-là.

Philippe s'exclame:

– Quoi? Tu as invité Aldo! Alors moi, je n'y vais pas. Je ne l'aime pas.

Pierre lui dit:

– Ça va, Okédou, ne t'énerve pas. C'est lui qui a voulu venir. Mais comme il n'est pas arrivé, on n'est pas obligé de l'attendre…

Philippe répond:

– Ok-dou! On s'en va.

Les enfants enfourchent leurs bicyclettes et laissent Margot derrière eux.

La petite s'assoit sur les marches de l'escalier devant la maison. Elle est triste. Encore une fois, ses frères l'ont mise de côté.

À ce moment, débouchant d'une ruelle, un petit garçon arrive tout essoufflé sur sa bicyclette.

# 3

## Un drôle de géant

Le garçon s'arrête à côté de Margot.

– Salut, je m'appelle Aldo. Les autres ne sont pas encore arrivés?

Margot a les yeux ronds. Est-ce que c'est vraiment lui, Aldo le géant? Ses frères se sont bien moqués. Aldo est plus petit qu'elle!

Elle répond:

– Ils sont partis. Ils ne t'ont pas attendu. Moi, je suis Margot, la sœur de Pierre, de Jean et de Jacques.

Aldo sourit tristement:

– J'étais sûr que ça se passerait comme ça. Ils ne veulent jamais jouer avec moi.

– Pourquoi? demande Margot.

– Parce que je suis plus petit. Tu vois bien, je suis de ta taille. Pourtant, j'ai dix ans.

Margot ne comprend pas:

– Alors, pourquoi disent-ils que tu es un géant?

– Parce que je m'appelle Aldo Legrand. Alors ils se moquent de moi. Mais s'ils savaient qui je suis vraiment, ils ne riraient plus…

– Que veux-tu dire?

– Peux-tu garder un secret, Margot?

– Bien sûr!

– Je suis un véritable géant.

– Pff! Tu es aussi menteur que mes frères.

– Mais non, je te jure que c'est vrai! Je

viens d'une famille de géants. Mon père est un géant, ma mère et mes sœurs sont des géantes.

Margot pense qu'il est fou.

– Je ne te crois pas. D'ailleurs, les géants, ça n'existe pas.

Aldo répond:

– Alors viens chez moi. Je vais te présenter ma famille. Tu verras bien que je dis la vérité.

Margot est d'accord. Plutôt que de s'ennuyer à la maison, aussi bien aller faire un tour avec Aldo. Même si c'est un drôle de menteur.

# Haute mère

La maison d'Aldo est dans un autre quartier.
Un quartier étrange que Margot ne connaît
pas. Les maisons sont plus anciennes et les
rues, plus étroites. Les arbres sont très hauts
et font beaucoup d'ombre.

Au bout d'un moment, Aldo stoppe sa
bicyclette et se tourne vers Margot:

– On approche. Pour arriver chez nous,
on doit passer entre ces deux vieilles maisons. L'herbe est trop haute pour pédaler, il
faut marcher. Suis-moi.

Ils appuient leurs bicyclettes contre le mur

d'une des maisons et s'engagent dans le sentier. C'est tellement embroussaillé que Margot doit parfois tenir la main d'Aldo pour ne pas le perdre de vue. Et il faut souvent se pencher pour éviter de recevoir des branches dans les yeux. Tout au bout, une grille barre le chemin. Aldo sort une clé de sa poche.

Il dit:

– Ici, c'est mon entrée secrète. Il n'y a que moi qui en ai la clé. Et tu es la première personne que j'amène chez moi.

En disant cela, Aldo ouvre la grille et pénètre dans un grand jardin plein d'arbres. Il n'y en a pas autant que dans une forêt, mais beaucoup quand même. Au fond du jardin, Margot aperçoit une immense maison de pierre surmontée d'une tour et d'une haute cheminée.

En approchant de la maison, Margot remarque quelque chose de bizarre: les marches de l'escalier sont anormalement hautes, plus hautes qu'elle-même. Jamais elle ne pourra monter cet escalier. Et puis, un râteau et une pelle de trois mètres de long sont appuyés contre un mur. Trois mètres! Et la porte d'entrée, elle doit bien faire six mètres de haut!

Margot ne sait plus quoi penser. Aldo disait peut-être la vérité quand il parlait de sa famille…

– Viens, Margot, lui dit Aldo. Pour monter, on passe par ici.

Il lui montre, sur le côté de l'escalier, une petite plate-forme de bois qui fonctionne

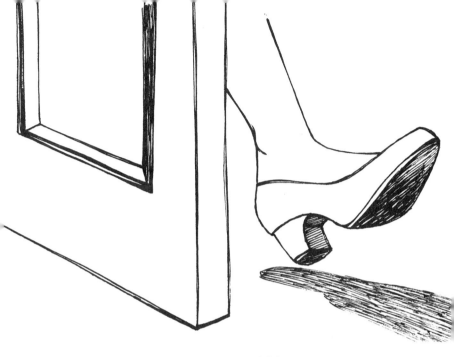

comme un ascenseur. Aldo tourne une
manivelle et un système de poulies les hisse
jusqu'à la porte d'entrée.

Aldo explique:

– Mes parents ont dû adapter un peu la
maison pour moi.

Sur ces mots, la porte s'ouvre et Margot
voit deux gigantesques pieds s'avancer. Elle

lève les yeux et aperçoit alors une grande,
une très grande personne. C'est une géante!
Elle doit mesurer dix fois la taille de Margot!

# 5
## Une très grande famille

La géante secoue un linge et de grosses miettes tombent comme de la grêle sur les deux enfants.

– Attention, maman, on est là! crie Aldo en se protégeant de ses bras.

Sa mère baisse la tête et dit en souriant:

– Oh! Mon Aldo, excuse-moi! Mais… tu as amené quelqu'un à ce que je vois!

La mère se penche et prend doucement Margot dans sa main:

– Bonjour. Je suis contente que mon fils ait une petite amie.

Margot tremble de partout.

En voyant les yeux apeurés de Margot, la mère la rassure:

– N'aie pas peur, ma belle, je ne mange pas les enfants!

La mère prend Aldo dans son autre main et emmène les deux enfants à l'intérieur.

Ébahie, Margot découvre une maison comme elle n'en a jamais vu. Les meubles, les fenêtres, la vaisselle, tout est démesurément grand. C'est vraiment une maison de géants. Pour s'asseoir sur une chaise, Margot aurait besoin d'un escabeau. D'ailleurs, une petite échelle de corde pend à l'une des chaises. C'est sûrement pour Aldo.

Tout à coup, deux autres géantes accourent dans la pièce. La maison vibre sous

leurs pas. Elles regardent Margot avec curio-
sité.

Aldo dit à Margot:

– Je te présente mes deux petites sœurs,
Carmen et Mona.

– Comment, petites! Mais elles sont im-
menses!

– C'est une façon de parler: elles sont plus
jeunes que moi.

La mère dépose Aldo et Margot au creux
d'un énorme coussin dans un profond sofa.

Carmen et Mona s'assoient de chaque côté.
Elles semblent très intéressées par la nouvelle
venue.

Margot demande:

– Pourquoi est-ce qu'Aldo n'est pas aussi
grand que vous?

Carmen répond:

– Aldo est, disons, un petit géant. Il est né comme ça. C'est pour ça qu'il peut aller à l'école avec les autres enfants. Autrement, il irait en Europe, à l'école des géants.

Aldo ajoute:

– Ça ne me dérange pas d'être petit. Je suis heureux quand même. Ma famille m'aime. Mais je n'ai pas beaucoup d'amis.

Margot lui dit:

– Moi, je peux être ton amie.

Aldo lui sourit.

La mère d'Aldo a servi une collation aux enfants.

Debout sur sa chaise, Margot contemple son morceau de gâteau. Il est gros comme une tente de camping!

Aldo explique:

– Ma mère a toujours un peu de difficulté avec les petites portions…

Carmen et Mona ont fini leur assiette.

Elles commencent à se tirailler.

La mère intervient:

– Doucement, les filles! Votre père dort.

Aldo se tourne vers Margot:

– Mon père travaille toute la nuit comme

garde forestier aux États-Unis. C'est pour ça qu'il dort le jour.

Margot demande:

– Aux États-Unis? Mais c'est loin! Est-ce qu'il y va tous les jours?

– Mon père a des bottes de sept lieues. En vingt minutes, il est rendu.

Margot fronce les sourcils. «Mais… mais, les bottes de sept lieues n'appartiennent-elles pas aux ogres?» pense-t-elle.

# 6

# L'ogre

À ce moment, les deux sœurs d'Aldo tombent de leurs chaises dans un vacarme épouvantable. Leurs pleurs et leurs cris résonnent dans toute la maison. Margot prie de tout son cœur pour que le bruit ne réveille pas le père.

Si c'était un ogre? C'est peut-être comme ça qu'ils font dans cette famille: Aldo attire les enfants dans la maison, l'ogresse leur sert de grosses collations, et quand les enfants sont bien dodus, l'ogre les mange. Mon Dieu! Il faut fuir à tout prix!

Margot se précipite pour descendre de sa chaise. Trop tard! la porte de la cuisine s'ouvre. Un géant barbu et fâché apparaît. Fronçant ses sourcils noirs, il voit Margot puis s'écrie:

– Qu'est-ce qui se passe ici?

L'ogre regarde sa femme:

– Qu'est-ce que ça veut dire, Maria? Tu donnes à manger aux souris, maintenant?

Aldo prend la défense de Margot:

– Ce n'est pas une souris, papa, c'est mon amie!

– Comment? dit son père en le voyant. Tu n'es pas à l'école, toi?

– Voyons, papa, c'est samedi!

Le géant fait «hmm» et s'approche de Margot, toute tremblante. Il la prend par le

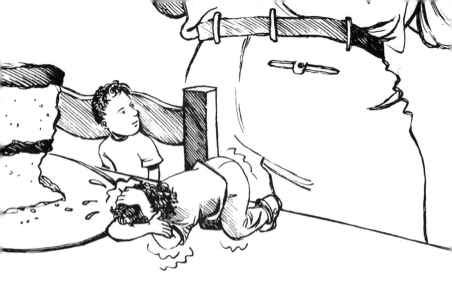

col de chemise et la dépose sur la table. De sa
grosse voix, il lui demande:

– Je te fais peur, hein?

Margot ne dit rien, elle se cache le visage
entre les mains. Elle sent ses cheveux tout
raides sur sa tête. Le géant se met à rire:

– Ha! Ha! Ha! Ça me rappelle de bons
souvenirs. De délicieux souvenirs, même.
Comme ça, tu es l'amie de mon fils? Bon,
alors je ne te mangerai pas… Ha! Ha! Ha!

Le père d'Aldo fait demi-tour et sort de la cuisine. La mère prend Margot dans sa main et la rassure:

– Ne t'en fais pas, ma belle, mon mari fait des blagues. Il ne mange plus les enfants. Depuis qu'il a lui-même des enfants, il a beaucoup changé. Il est devenu végétarien.

Aldo voit bien que Margot n'est qu'à moitié rassurée. Il lui dit:

– Viens, on va monter dans la plus haute tour de la maison. De la fenêtre, on a une vue superbe, on peut voir jusqu'à la rivière.

Margot demande:

– Crois-tu qu'on puisse voir mes frères au pique-nique? Je sais qu'ils se rendaient dans un parc, près de la rivière.

Margot aimerait bien les rejoindre. Maintenant, elle voudrait quitter la maison des géants. Elle ne s'y sent pas très en sécurité.

# 7

# Alerte sur la rivière

Aldo et Margot grimpent l'un après l'autre tous les petits escaliers bâtis à même les hautes marches de la tour. Arrivés tout en haut, ils se hissent jusqu'à la fenêtre. On voit très loin, en effet. Aldo tend une paire de jumelles à Margot:

– Tiens, tu verras mieux.

Margot scrute les environs. Elle reconnaît les rues autour de sa maison, puis les parcs. Soudain, elle voit son frère Jean, et Jacques, et Léa-la-frisée. Mais que se passe-t-il? Ils ont l'air affolés!

Margot tente de comprendre. Elle voit un attroupement se former près de l'eau. Mon Dieu! Quelqu'un est tombé dans la rivière! Elle le reconnaît, c'est Okédou. Mais il ne sait pas nager.

Margot s'écrie:

– Okédou se noie! Okédou se noie!

Margot et Aldo redescendent l'escalier à toute vitesse. Il faut faire quelque chose! Et il faut surtout le faire vite! Aldo ne voit qu'une solution: enfiler les bottes de son père. Mais acceptera-t-il de lui prêter ses précieuses bottes de sept lieues? Aldo court jusqu'à la chambre de ses parents.

Son père a tout entendu. Il ouvre la porte et lui tend les fameuses bottes:

– Prends-les, mon garçon. Tu es assez

grand… enfin, je veux dire que tu as l'âge de prendre tes responsabilités. Vite! Va sauver ton copain!

Aldo est tout ému:

– Oh! Merci, papa!

Margot ne comprend rien à ce qui se passe. Elle s'énerve:

– Mais il faut appeler la police, les pompiers, voyons! Okédou se noie!

Elle n'a pas le temps de finir sa phrase qu'Aldo la met sur ses épaules. Il est devenu aussi fort qu'un géant! Les bottes de sept lieues, une fois à ses pieds, ont rapetissé à sa taille. Il dit:

– Avec les bottes de mon père, nous serons là en cinq secondes. Ce sont des bottes magiques.

Ils sortent de la maison. Margot entend à peine le géant crier à son fils:

– Sois prudent, mon grand!

Ils sont déjà rendus deux rues plus loin. Un pas de plus et ils sont tout près de chez Margot. Un dernier pas et les voilà tous les deux à l'entrée du parc.

Aldo dépose Margot encore tout étourdie et cache ses grandes bottes dans un buisson. Il court jusqu'au bord de l'eau. C'est la pagaille! Tout le monde veut sauver Okédou, mais personne ne sait très bien nager…

Sans perdre un instant, Aldo plonge. Il nage jusqu'à Okédou qui est sur le point d'être englouti pour de bon, le prend sur son dos et le ramène jusqu'à la rive.

Pierre, Jean et Jacques aident les deux garçons à se hisser hors de l'eau.

Okédou tousse et crache, mais il est hors

de danger. Il regarde le petit géant dans les
yeux et dit:

– Aldo, tu m'as sauvé la vie!

# Retour au pique-nique

Tout le monde entoure Aldo et le félicite. Margot est très excitée. Elle dit:

– Il est courageux, hein, mon ami Aldo? Mais c'est aussi grâce à moi si Okédou est sauf. C'est moi qui l'ai vu de la fenêtre.

Son frère Jean lui demande:

– Qu'est-ce que tu racontes? De quelle fenêtre parles-tu?

Margot répond:

– La fenêtre de la maison d'Aldo, la maison des géants! Moi, je suis allée chez Aldo. C'est une vraie famille de géants. On a mangé du gâteau haut comme ça, et sa mère, elle m'a prise dans sa main et elle m'a soulevée dans les airs. Et puis, on est venus avec les bottes magiques de son père et...

À ce moment, elle s'aperçoit que tous les enfants la regardent comme si elle avait perdu la raison.

Aldo rit:

– Tu as beaucoup d'imagination, Margot!

Puis il explique aux autres:

– Margot est venue chez moi, et on a regardé un film de monstres et de géants.

Margot sent les larmes qui lui montent aux yeux. Pourquoi Aldo ne leur dit-il pas la vérité? Elle n'a pas inventé toute cette histoire, tout de même!